HOLY MARRIAGE, HAPPY MARRIAGE

Holy Marriage, Happy Marriage

Faith-Filled Ways to a Better Relationship

CHRIS AND LINDA PADGETT

servant

AN IMPRINT OF
FRANCISCAN MEDIA
Cincinnati, Ohio

Library of Congress Cataloging-in-Publication Data
Padgett, Chris, 1970-
Holy marriage, happy marriage : faith-filled ways to a better relationship /
Chris and Linda Padgett.
pages cm
Includes bibliographical references and index.
ISBN 978-1-61636-892-0 (alk. paper)
1. Marriage—Religious aspects—Catholic Church. I. Title.
BX2250.P3155 2015
248.8'44—dc23
2015019403

ISBN 978-1-61636-892-0

Published by Servant, an imprint of Franciscan Media
28 W. Liberty St.
Cincinnati, OH 45202
www.FranciscanMedia.org

Printed in the United States of America.
Printed on acid-free paper.
15 16 17 18 19 5 4 3 2 1

Contents

I've been married to Linda so long, I can sit in the same room with her, not saying a word, and still know I've done something wrong.

Now that I have your attention, let me just say that I love being married. I always tell people who are considering marriage that the secret to a happy relationship is to "marry up." Most guys who have working marriages can readily agree with me that their wives are the reason for their marital success. Linda and I have spent a lot of time leading marriage retreats, and I have taught a class on Christian marriage at the local university for numerous years—and we think we have a few tips for those interested in improving their marriages.

Today, more than ever, we need to be reminded why marriage matters. For many couples, marriage is something that seems broken beyond repair. They have truly "lost that lovin' feeling" (how could I not have a *Top Gun* reference?), and the classic "ball and chain" marital cliché is more applicable than they would like to admit. Is there hope for marriage? How can couples not only survive the traps that are collapsing marriages, but truly thrive in these difficult times?

We believe there is a way out of the marriage mess many spouses have found themselves trapped within, but it will take a new way of thinking, a new strategy for living, and a new level of commitment. This book is not simply for marriages that are struggling; rather, it is for all marriages. And we think the advice given here is practical and helpful for both newly-weds and those who have been together for decades.

St. John Paul II loved marriage. His document *Familiaris Consortio* emphasizes the holy opportunity Christians have in living out their vocations. This apostolic exhortation says that a marriage that is truly functional does three very important things. First, a holy marriage will witness to the world a relational structure that can endure all things. We allude to this, even as a secular society, when we echo the vows, "in good times and bad, richer or poorer, in sickness and in health, until death do us part." When a marriage is truly working, enduring any circumstance with generosity and sacrifice, the impact of this relational structure bespeaks the commitment of our God. When someone who is outside of the Church looks at the respect and dignity of Catholic married couples, they can find hope. In a time when relationships are unsteady, fickle, and falling apart, holy marriage can breathe new life into the world's perspective of marriage by its willingness to stand amidst great opposition.

The second thing that *Familiaris Consortio* emphasizes about a healthy marriage is that it is a witness of Jesus's love for the Church. We are the bride of Christ, and the greatest declaration of the groom's love is found at the cross. The complete gift of self by Jesus at Calvary is so entire that it is life-giving. From the side of Christ, the blood and water flow, and the Church is born. The bride of Christ is birthed from the sword-pierced side of our Savior, and in many ways it reminds the reader of the Scriptures, where Eve is made from the side of Adam in the Garden of Eden. When a husband willingly lays down his life for his bride, and when a woman gives herself entirely to her husband, new life is brought forth.

The third truth we find emphasized in *Familiaris Consortio* is that a society is changed for the better when a marriage is working. We certainly value sacrificial behavior in our sports, employment, and academics, but it is of a most lasting impact when it is found within marriage. The sacrificial and service orientation of spouses within marriage mirrors the love that God has within the Triune Godhead, and this resonates within the social structure of a world that has so often lost its way.

This book is about the importance of the sacrament of marriage, from the perspective of an ordinary couple living out their vocation in a less than ordinary time. Our culture has lost its vision of marriage's sanctity, and the unfortunate unraveling of the holy bond within the Christian milieu is all too common. We need to be reminded of why we believe marriage to be a lasting pillar in the human experience, why it is a sacrament, and why it is worth fighting for.

Linda and I have been married for more than twenty-three years, have nine kids, and still seem to like each other. We will share in this book the reasons why the Church sticks strongly to the sacrament of marriage, why it is important for the human experience, and how you can move forward in your journey of sacrificial and service-oriented love toward your spouse.

You'll find here a lot of personal stories, as well as numerous Scripture and Church references about marriage. We hope and pray that you enjoy this labor of love—and that you find new ways to cherish your own marriage once again.

—Chris Padgett

Prelude

The landscape of marriage and family is very diverse today, and there are many reasons for this. We will try to make a brief mention of some family variables that different readers will have, keeping in mind that some people who purchase this book will have already had marriages end in divorce or death, while some have just recently gotten engaged and are hoping to start out on the right foot. While we can't fix what has already been broken, knowing why we have struggles and what makes our marriages so unique can help.

We will look at a few of the common factors couples have as they come into marriage and explore some of the reasons why we approach things the way we do. This is a book that would have been very helpful for us when we first got married, since most of the resources then were pretty outdated and seemed to be unrealistic. But this book is also very practical and informative for those who, like us today, have been married for quite some time. What we are saying is that, wherever you are on your marriage journey, you're going to love this book!

Some Common Factors

Marriage has regularly been respected and found to be essential in most every culture throughout time, yet there are things anyone getting married will have to tackle. Here are a few of them:

Preconceived Ideas about Marriage. Usually, both people have an idea of what a marriage is supposed to look like. In the past, it was what they saw modeled by their parents, but today the media and certainly Hollywood are instead laying a foundation for the couple at an early age, setting expectations for not only the big day itself, but for marital life. This needs to be addressed even before the couple say "I do" in order to have a healthy marriage.

Our Brokenness, Weakness, and Emptiness (Baggage). Every man and woman entering into marriage brings a lot more to the union than clothes and furnishings. Each person has a past, and skeletons hidden in the closet have an uncanny way of making appearances at very awkward moments. Spouses need to be aware of the lives lived before they are united in matrimony if they plan to have a marriage that endures the test of time.

Societal and Religious Expectations. Every marriage is impacted by societal and religious expectations, even if the couple does not adhere to those religious tenets. If you are Catholic and suddenly decide to marry someone who is Jewish, we can guarantee that you will find yourself having certain difficult conversations with extended family members. If you are in a society that places a lot of importance on your elders, and you suddenly have a ceremony without their being given proper respect, it is going to cause a certain amount of distress.

Family Dynamics (Overbearing in-laws, Role of Extended Family, Location). This issue is certainly very obvious to anyone who is married, and you would do well to consider this if you have not yet set the date. Your ignorance of the many family pressures and numerous variables will not change your love for each other, but it is worth recognizing and discussing together so that you can be united against known difficulties.

Different Personalities (Type A / Easygoing). Notice we didn't say *multiple* personalities. We all have a different way that we approach life, and this is very true within marriages. No matter where you're from, you don't always approach life in the same way as your spouse just because you are married and living under the same roof. These differences of personalities are very important to understand when you look into and work to live out the beauty of marriage.

Dreams and Goals. Often it is the sharing of dreams and goals that can unite a couple in the first place, and as you will read later in this book, we consider this a very important virtue to continue to foster if you want your marriage to be a success. It is true and good to pursue some common dreams, regardless of your religion, financial status, or age.

Expectations of the Role of the Feminine/Masculine. This can be a factor in every culture. Often the differences in man/woman roles explain why certain struggles are found in marriages.

All of these factors can be evident in *any* marriage—Christian or not. But how will the common factors of marriage be better understood within the context of Christianity? In this book, you will see that there is grace and beauty in the way that Christ has an impact within marriage and family. First and foremost, our Christian faith places these factors within a context of love, which often gives great potential for sanctity in otherwise difficult scenarios.

Avoiding Stereotypes

Finally, although there are common factors that can affect marriages, it is important not to fall into stereotypes and clichés that may have a negative impact on the journey of a marital couple. What will help in our discussion of successful marriages is not a bumper-sticker spirituality, but something solid and proven, even in this day and age of gadgets and gimmicks. We surely can think of a few stereotypes concerning marriage that do not hold much weight in helping a couple endure the test of time.

One such example of a stereotype in marriage is the family comparison: a man marrying someone like his mother and a woman wanting to marry a man like her father. Now, my wife is wonderfully capable and independent, and so is my mother, but that may be where most similarities end. And I can see very little about me in Linda's father, except a tenacious and ferocious love for my family. Sometimes I wonder if we simply use this example as an excuse for lazy behavior.

A mother who was so nurturing, loving, and quiet, all the while keeping a perfectly clean house, is certainly wonderful, but her approach may not work for your wife who now has seven boys who feel it is their duty to unfold each linen, unpack each drawer, and understandably drive their mother crazy. A father who was capable of fixing every broken faucet, bike, or boo-boo and still playing catch in the afternoons may have been a wonderful gift to you as a child, but this may be an almost impossible expectation for your husband, who is not mechanically inclined and has to work two jobs in order to make ends meet. Your family unit is unique to your experience, and family comparisons can become difficult to uphold. Stereotypes usually do more harm than good.

Another stereotype that couples often fall into is the false notion that certain domains and tasks are for one gender and not the other. Her place is in the kitchen and laundry room, while his place is in the garage and workplace. This is advocated by both the media and some couples, and it can be divisive and detrimental to a couple's growth. For a husband to decidedly insist that he will not change a baby's diaper because that is a job for a woman is basically an excuse for selfishness. It may be a couple's pattern that the husband works, the wife has the dinner ready for him when he comes home, and he relaxes with a drink in front of the television while she cleans up, but this isn't usually a recipe for success.

In my home, I'll cook the food if it is a grilling night, and not because my wife is incapable of doing such a manly job! Actually she helps me put the thing together. I should rephrase this: I help her put it together. Actually, she put most of it together, and I think my daughter's boyfriend helped. Okay, so maybe I was watching television when it was being prepared. The point is, the question shouldn't be whether something is a man's job or a woman's job; rather, the question should be about what needs to be done and how a spouse can help. It's all about serving each other and our families.

Of course, sometimes this works better than others. I remember once when my father came to visit, he wanted me to help him unload the dishwasher so my wife didn't have that on her list of things to do. We both managed to get everything into a cupboard and drawer—a routine that happened for a few days. When my father left my wife told me that I wasn't allowed to do the dishes because the last few days had resulted in her not being able to find a single item in her kitchen when she needed it!

In our family, Linda rarely likes to drive if I am home. In fact, her comment has been: "I have the babies, you drive the car." We have kept with that philosophy over the years, especially since I am unable to trade places with her. But this doesn't mean that driving is only a man's job or that she doesn't drive; in fact she does so constantly. The point is, a husband always need to be asking himself: "How can I help my wife?" It is all about giving of ourselves and about making the family work and function in a manner that flows with our goals and dreams.

The final example of stereotypes couples can fall into is the odd idea that a good marriage is one where the union is between two unlikely people because opposites attract. When I was young, Lyle Lovett married Julia Roberts, and I think the question the entire world was asking was: "Really? What does she see in him?" We all knew what he saw in her, but good grief.

Yes, there are certainly times when two people who are truly opposites find that their relationship just works. Possibly they see in the other qualities they wish they had in themselves, or they find an admirable quality and character that is out of their reach. In many relationships, one person balances the other with gifts the other doesn't have, but again, you don't have to be opposites in order for this dynamic to be present or for a marriage to succeed. The goal should be a mutual complementarity that is intended by one toward the other for their benefit.

So let's shatter these stereotypes on the way to building healthier marriages.

If you want a marriage to last, you cannot ask your husband to be like your father. You can't expect your wife to do all the things for you your mother did when you were a child. It is all about you two becoming a singular unit, a body that is fluid and functioning together for a single purpose.

Standing adamantly against something or for something because that is what a man or a woman does is a way to demean your spouse and foster a selfishness that marriage must do without. If you truly want your marriage to thrive, you have to work together, love and grow together, even if it means trying something a little different—like vacuuming the house!

Overall, the complementarity of a man and a woman, with her strengths aiding his weaknesses, and his strengths filling in hers, is the gift you both become to one another daily. If you approach marriage with a heart of mutual self-giving, it will smooth over your rough edges and fill in your empty places. Marriage lasts because of an effort by both parties to work together, with heaven in mind.

Part One

A New Way of Thinking

There are a lot of people who seem awfully unhappy in marriage. Even some of the "good ones'" seem like they are on borrowed time. Have you ever spent time with a couple that at first glance appears to have the right stuff to make it, but after awhile you realize there are little cracks in the foundation of the marriage that, if left untended over time, will end up destroying the union? Marriage needs to be built on selfless love—and on a firm foundation. As Alice von Hildebrand says, "Marriage calls each spouse to fight against himself for the sake of his beloved. This is why it has become so unpopular today. People are no longer willing to achieve the greatest of all victories, the victory over self."[1]

Chris

When I was a small child, my grandparents would spend their winter vacations on Melbourne Beach, Florida. It was very common for my sister and me to fly out of freezing South Dakota to go and visit them on holiday. I can remember walking along the rubbery grass at their particular beach home, seeing a coral snake for the first time. Those were the days of Polaroid cameras and trips to the Kennedy Space Station, which, albeit very informative, was pretty boring to a young child. Truth be told, I wanted Disney. The sand on the east coast of Florida is generally not as soft as it is on the west, but let me state that any sand in Florida was better than the dirt of the Great Plains, which was buried under ice and snow from October to March!

We used to have those old plastic buckets and little shovels you could build sand castles with. I was never one for sand sculptures, nor was I much of an engineer. Usually, my constructs would last for a brief period of time, only to be swept away by the incoming waves. In all honesty, I was not building something to last; I just wanted to have some fun and see what might happen if I built a moat here or added another mountain of sand there. My guess is that most children build sand castles just for the moment at hand. When we get older, we usually help our kids make the sand castles, or watch with one eye on our children and the other on our latest beach read. And after our outings at the beach, we go back to a home that is *not* made of sand or placed next to the crashing waves—one that ideally is so solidly built that it can weather any of the storms the area may encounter. Sand castles are fine for the beach, but when it comes to real life, we want to reside in something that lasts.

Many a marriage is approached as if it is just some experiment that is bound to work because the conditions are correct, the moment is ideal, and everyone seems to be having fun. But when the waves crash in after the initial honeymoon phase, or when storms arise with unexpected destruction, many marriages are washed away because they are not built on a firm foundation. Of course, few couples think they are unprepared for marriage once the big day arrives. No one usually concludes that they need more pre-Cana classes; rather, they are more likely worried about finances for the wedding and honeymoon, or who is and isn't attending the ceremony. Most couples certainly don't intend to set their marriages to fail, yet it is no surprise that some marriages end up being disastrous.

With that said, we believe there is still hope for couples who have started out on the wrong foot, having built their marriage on a shifting foundation. There are some key things that can be done, but both parties have to be willing to do what it takes. Both must realize that God wants their marriage to be a success and is capable of solidifying what seems impossibly unstable. There is a big difference in a marriage that has been crafted and joined together by God and one that has been thrown together by man. "What therefore God has joined together, let not man put asunder" (Mark 10:9).

There will always be storms in a marriage, but your marriage can be built to last if it is entered into with love, built on solid principles, and truly given over to Christ. Remember, Jesus is a carpenter, after all!

Many people have embraced a false way of thinking when it comes to marriage. Through the years, we have found there to be eight basic qualities that every marriage needs to embrace in order to thrive and not simply survive. Using examples from our own marriage, this book will look at each of these qualities, addressing the false way couples implement them and suggesting a new way of thinking that can help any couple's relationship journey back into health.

Chapter One

Freedom

The first basic quality of a solid marriage is freedom. We
will each speak about this attribute, and you will notice
that it is connected to the theological virtue of charity. Love
cannot be expressed without freedom, and freedom is truly not
authentic without love.

Linda

A marriage based in love and trust should be filled with
freedom. Without it, frustration will build up and fear will
become the ruling emotion in the house. Each spouse should be
free to fully be themselves, and together their marriage should
be free to be unique from other relationships.

I married a man who was voted "Most Unique Personality"
his senior year in high school. Through our years of marriage,
he has never failed to live up to that title. I have come to learn
that the different ways in which he processes a situation or
deals with conflict are his version of normal. Even though I
occasionally get frustrated because he does things differently
than I do, I have learned to give Chris the freedom to be himself.

Thankfully, this freedom goes both ways. Chris has learned
that I take longer than he does to cool off after an argument.

He knows that "Sorry" will eventually come; I just need time. Chris has also learned to give me the freedom to pursue my crazy dreams and sometimes extravagant projects because he knows I ultimately do what I do for the benefit and enjoyment of our family. In the same way I have learned to accept his compulsion to collect the things he loves—whether books or tattoos—and his crazy need to check and re-check light switches in the house, his patience with me gives me the freedom to be who I am.

Too often people enter marriage hoping to eventually change their spouse. They want to see them more organized, more financially responsible, more expressive with their love, or simply more outgoing and social. But the real conflict comes when they realize they are not being accepted for who they are. We must seek to understand our loved ones rather than change them into the image *we* want to see.

Another point to make is that people also change as they get older. Both Chris and I have gone through many adaptations through the years. At different times we have pursued new interests or tried new ways of doing things that neither one of us would have considered in our early years of marriage. But that's okay. When we first got married, there was no way to fully understand the depth of our own hearts and minds, let alone the depth of each other's. As we age, we learn more about ourselves. We mature and begin to look at life differently as new things take priority.

It is a blessing in our marriage that we have allowed each other to evolve and change. Chris didn't marry a woman who was a health freak and wanted chickens in her backyard. I didn't marry a man who had tattoos or enjoyed hunting. If we had not given each other the freedom to grow and discover aspects of ourselves, we would have missed a lot of adventure in our marriage. The bottom line for me—and the truth that allows me to give Chris that freedom—is the fact that I trust him. I am certain of his love for me and for our family, and I know he ultimately wants to bless us and provide for us. Therefore I can give him the freedom to experiment with new ideas and interests, and even join him in his new obsessions, because we are in this together.

In addition to giving each other the freedom to be themselves, each couple as a whole should feel the freedom to be unique. Comparison is a dangerous practice. Each marriage—and each family—is different from any other marriage or family. The trouble comes when comparison causes discontentment and judgment. Our marriage certainly does not resemble the marriages of others. The way we act with each other and show our love for each other might not be understood by onlookers. But we are not required to satisfy other people with our relationship; we just need to be ourselves in our own version of a happy marriage.

Once you start having a family, comparison becomes more difficult to avoid. We see other people's kids being so well-behaved and polite. It often seems that other families have it all together. We look at a couple and say, "Man, that's not fair. They have perfect children. They must have a lot of money to afford that beautiful house. They are so in love. And to top it off, they are both in perfect shape." But, the truth is, we never know what really goes on in another family.

My favorite quote for those moments of comparison was given to me by a neighbor years ago. She didn't even know the source of the quote, but it has been a keeper. Here it is: "Don't judge the inside of your house by the outside of another." It's unfair to compare all the dirtiness you see in your own marriage and family to the pristine image of someone else's. Each marriage and family has issues that need to be addressed. You should not assume you are the only one who struggles.

There is great peace in being yourself. It's hard to have the courage at times, but I think it's much more difficult living under the self-judgment of comparison. When we first moved to Steubenville, Ohio, the first families we met had daughters who wore long skirts instead of pants. Coming from Florida, our children were used to wearing shorts and jeans on a regular basis. I was afraid we had moved into a neighborhood that would judge us for a lack of holiness based on what we wore.

A week into living in our new house, we were invited to a neighborhood party, and my daughters asked me if they should put on skirts to attend the party. I was tempted to say yes. I didn't want our new neighbors to judge us, and I didn't want my children to feel like they didn't fit in. However, I am pretty stubborn. I told my girls to put on jeans. I said, "Our new neighbors will accept us for who we are or we are going to freak out their world." It turned out that our neighbors were not at all like I thought they might be. Even though they had chosen a standard for their own families, they were not judging us for ours. Within days, our children found other families that also wore pants and shorts, and we became a natural fit in the neighborhood, where every family was practicing their version of life.

Love is freeing. Loving your spouse as they are and allowing them to grow and learn at their own pace is a great gift. Freedom to be who we are and the couple or family we are called to become is possible when spouses extend that trust to each other.

Chris

Every marriage must be grounded in freedom. I have connected this initial quality for marital success with the theological virtue of love, for you cannot truly love without freedom. However, when we look at this basic, foundational attribute, we need to make sure our definition of freedom is the same as God's. Let's look at the false perspective first.

False Perspective

For many people in our world today, freedom means doing what I want, where I want, and with whomever I want. The world says this independence is true freedom—and unfortunately this false perspective seeps into many marriages. The Catholic Church says that the impact of such a false perspective upon a marriage is very negative:

> At the root of these negative phenomena there frequently lies a corruption of the idea and the experience of freedom, conceived not as a capacity for

realizing the truth of God's plan for marriage and the family, but as an autonomous power of self-affirmation, often against others, for one's own selfish well-being.[2]

Many people are under the delusion that they should always gratify their desires—that saying no is really stifling what it means to be free. When a couple enters into marriage, this inability to have every passion satisfied seems to restrict their God-given freedom. Think of it like this: If you have practiced doing what you want, when you want, with whomever you want for your whole life, it is going to be difficult to stifle those tendencies and inclinations to say no to self-gratification later in life.

What is the motivation to say no? Well, when a couple says yes to marriage, this is their motivation to be monogamous. This works for many marriages for a certain period of time, but when the storms come in the following years—or the cute little quirk one spouse loved in the other one when they were dating becomes the most annoying quality any human being has ever had—couples begin to reevaluate the idea of freedom. *Why do I have to put up with this annoying trait in my spouse? Why do I have to stop doing this, when I've done this certain thing during our whole relationship? Why can't my spouse just stop doing what drives me so crazy? It's like my spouse is intentionally doing this to spite me!* The longer we follow this path, the more the questions regarding our freedom being infringed upon become applicable. Freedom in marriages where the foundations have these cracks of discontent, stifled passions, and inconsiderate spouses seems to be in jeopardy, if not entirely lost.

How to get freedom back? Many give ultimatums that insist the spouse change—or else. He or she didn't marry a person who did this. Or one spouse points out that the other has changed; the relationship isn't the same as it used to be. This tendency to give ultimatums and demand changes is not conducive to freedom in a relationship. Freedom isn't about us getting things whenever we want.

Freedom is willingly making a choice to do something that will result in our sanctity. Freedom is walking toward acts and events that enable us to become saints. Freedom is what makes us truly alive, and that is not always found in doing what we want. Let's say a couple is having a nice, romantic dinner when suddenly the husband does that weird, annoying sucking-food-from-his-teeth thing that causes his wife to cringe. The wife is free to yell and scream about her husband's lack of consideration, especially since she's asked him to stop countless times. The freedom is there, but acting on that free moment could result in great pains of regret and frustration.

Here is a better example, one from real life. One day I was dropped off at a hotel after doing an event. The day had been lengthy, and I was exhausted and facing an early flight out the next morning. As I made my way toward my hotel room, carrying my guitar, three inebriated ladies crossed my path. They were not terribly unattractive, and they seemed to be having quite a bit of fun laughing and heading for one of the countless parties going on in the hotel that evening. As I walked by, one of them said: "Hey, I'll dance for you if you play a song for me." I got a bit nervous and mumbled something about my guitar being broken and proceeded to my room at a quicker pace. I could have freely pursued this avenue with one or all three of the women. I'm pretty sure there were some options available to me, but here is what I know: If I had pursued that moment under the guise of freedom, I would have lost everything that mattered to me, not the least of which was my integrity! Freedom has consequences, and you can ask any military veteran what he risked in fighting for you to have the freedom you possess. With this in mind, there is a new way of thinking that we must embrace. It is part of the foundation necessary for a good marriage.

A New Way of Thinking

We are free to love, not to use. We are free to die to self, not to gratify ourselves (see CCC, 1731).

Each family is unique. As Linda said: "Don't judge the inside of your house by the outside of another." We must walk in the freedom of our individual reflection of God's love. This corresponds to the theological virtue of love. In the eyes of the Church, marriage has to be agreed to and entered into with both parties being free to marry. Not simply free civilly, but also mentally and ecclesiastically. You obviously cannot be married to someone else, and simply having a divorce doesn't qualify one as being free to marry, ecclesiastically speaking. You have to be free to marry, and that may necessitate going through an annulment process to validate that your marriage wasn't authentic in the Church's eyes in the first place. You have to be free even mentally and emotionally.

Many of the reasons annulments are granted because of one person's psychological hindrances in freely assenting to marriage and what it entails. Real love is never forced, duped, or coerced. Real love can't be manufactured or manipulated. You are invited to love the way that God loves, which is life-giving. I think the disconnection between love and freedom causes confusion in our day and age. Love must have freedom to become, to grow, to endure. Freedom must have love to last.

I have been a man of many mistakes and issues, and yet Linda remains freely by my side. Her love, demonstrated in her free act of staying with me, is a picture of God, who is faithful and committed to us even when we fail. She is not forced to be with me, which makes her presence alongside me all the sweeter. In many ways, I wish that couples could get back to the simple fact that they are making a commitment to one another because it is the place that they can best live life to the full. What was it like for you when you first met? Did you feel like you had to be with one another? No! You wanted to be with one another. What changed? Is it possible that there were parts of your life that felt stifled and hindered? What freedom can you extend to one another in order to grow?

Activity

Ask yourself: "Are there outside influences hindering my freedom to be the version of the couple we want to be? What are they?"

As a couple, pray together for one another that each of you can freely become the beautiful saints you are called to be. Ask for forgiveness for the times you have hindered your spouse's freedom by your selfishness.

Chapter Two

Respect and Dignity

The second basic quality of a solid marriage is respect and dignity. We often treat friends and even strangers with more dignity and respect than our spouses. This attribute of dignity and respect connects to the cardinal virtue of justice. Justice is giving to God and to man the dignity and respect they deserve. Your spouse deserves your respect and dignity.

Linda

Respect is regularly easier to bestow on those to whom we are not related. Too often we pour out respect on bosses, celebrities, or neighbors who may not even live up to our high opinions of them, while we criticize and disrespect those individuals who have avowed themselves to us forever. Quite honestly, our spouses and children hold the singular most important place in the hierarchy of who should be treated with utmost dignity. Why? Because we are united to them through love and covenant more than any other people. They are the primary instruments God will use to make us holy.

Respect is the means by which we give dignity to our spouses. In fact, you cannot show dignity without showing respect. But exactly how do we do that? First, we show respect by the way we speak *to* our spouse. Second, we show respect by the way we speak *about* our spouse.

The Bible speaks about the power of the tongue (Proverbs 18:21). That little body part can cause permanent damage to the self-worth of an individual and wreak a mess of hurt in a marriage. Therefore, the way we speak to our husband/wife is crucial. Even though respect is not always communicated best through the nice words we speak, disrespect is definitely communicated very clearly in the hurtful words we speak. In those heated moments of disagreement, it is too easy to cross the line, slip into a downright mean tone, and say things we really don't feel. Then, when those extremely mean things are spoken too often, they become permanently scarred on the other's heart and can even become a real feeling in the heart of the speaker.

There has to be a line that does not get crossed. Early in our marriage, Chris and I promised each other that the word *divorce* would never be used. We knew that oftentimes couples use the threat of divorce during an argument as leverage or manipulation. But we also knew that the word spoken too much, even if we don't really mean it, could plant the seed that could eventually grow into a reality in our marriage. For us, the word *divorce* was just off limits.

By the time a couple gets married, they usually already know the other's hot buttons. We know what discussion topics will set our spouses off and hurt them the most—the way they look, the money they make, their past, or their weaknesses— so we must promise ourselves and each other that we will not go anywhere near those areas. Always respect your spouse enough to speak with kindness and love, avoiding the places that wound.

The second way we should show respect and dignity to our spouses is in the way we speak about them, especially to our family, our children, and our friends. We have all seen the stereotypical scenario where the wife is venting all of her frustrations concerning her husband to her mother. Or, how about those nights out with the guys where there is a litany of criticisms concerning "the old ball and chain"? Of course, television is full of scenes where the spouse is undermined in the presence of the children. These are all recipes for absolute failure in a marriage.

Though there may be times in which seeking the counsel of another person is necessary, it is best to keep the struggles and disagreements between the ones involved. Not only is it damaging to the relationship between your spouse and the ones you are talking to, especially in the case of parents and children, but it also feeds discontentment and bitterness in your own hearts as a couple. If you say something often enough, it can very well lead to truly feeling that way. Negativity breeds negativity.

Words hold so much power. We can use them to tear down our spouses, displaying disrespect and undermining their dignity, or we can work to build them up using words of love and encouragement. We must remember that our spouse holds the highest place in our hearts and lives, second only to God, and thus deserves all the respect we can give them.

Chris

Have you ever heard a couple argue? There is something very disheartening when you stumble into the middle of a heated conversation or hear someone fighting in another room. It feels awkward because it *is* awkward. Even those little jabs that seem to be done in play but are terribly barbed are usually not missed by innocent bystanders who pretend that nothing strange is happening.

I would like to connect these attributes of respect and dignity to the cardinal virtue of justice. Justice is giving God and man what they deserve. We go to church and worship and adore our God, and we treat others with dignity and respect simply because they are human beings. Doing this is obeying the most basic commandment: "You shall love the Lord your God with all your heart, and with all your soul, and with all your strength, and with all your mind; and your neighbor as yourself" (Luke 10:27). When couples begin to stray away from the basic practice of treating one another with dignity and respect, there are bound to be problems in the marriage.

When Linda and I first started dating, I can remember hearing the harsh way her father spoke to her mother. While they remained married until he eventually passed away, I often wondered how a husband could say those things to his wife and still remain together. Surely the bickering and volatile words were not what their relationship began with, but how did that eventually become the norm?

False Perspective

One example of a false perspective in marriage is the idea that I will respect you if you respect me. I will treat you with dignity if you do the same toward me. This is what happens to most marriages in conflict over time. We begin to take one another for granted and then take personal offense when our spouse does not do what it is we expect them to do. No longer is it just "He simply forgot"; rather, it becomes, "He doesn't respect my requests and is doing this on purpose." Marriage provides both the greatest opportunity for demonstrating respect to another human being and the greatest opportunity for disrespecting that person. The reason this that we know the numerous goods and potential of our spouse, and we can recognize when their full efforts are lacking in a particular matter. Instead of giving to them the benefit of the doubt, which we so often do in the workplace, to a stranger, or even to a family member we don't often see, we assume that our spouse, of all people, should be different. Do you take it personally when your boss doesn't bring you a coffee when you arrive at work? Of course not. Do you take offense when the grocery clerk doesn't ask you if you've had a bad day? No. For those who unintentionally offend us and ignore our feeling, we usually extend a bit of leeway. And yet we are so quick to attack, call our spouses on their offenses, note the hurts, and point out the inadequacies— because our spouses and therefore should know better on all accounts.

The problem with this line of thinking is that you will never consistently get the exact response from your spouse that you are looking for. You will always have something to complain about if you look, and you will always feel like you've told them before about that quirk that is so annoying. Your spouse may have days, weeks, or months when he or she seems to be tracking with you, but inevitably something happens and you move away from being the priority in your spouse's thoughts and actions. While having a little understanding of a particular situation may help explain the inadequate actions of your spouse, it won't change him or her, nor will it necessarily make you feel much better. What we all need is a new way of thinking.

A New Way of Thinking

Remember, your spouse is made in God's image and likeness. As stated, this connects with the cardinal virtue of justice: to give to God and man that which they are due. In the end, we must take responsibility for the way we respond to others. All we have to do is look back at the Garden of Eden to realize that we would prefer to blame someone else rather than accept responsibility for our actions. Think of Adam and Eve from the Genesis account and you can easily see the daily scenarios of life unfold. We have been given the perfect helpmate (this is our mindset from the start of marriage), a gift from God, with whom we will begin our new life together. The complementarity is perfect. No other person or thing can compare with the gift of our spouse—that is, until conflict occurs.

When we look at the Garden of Eden, Adam was told to tend and keep that which he had been given. He was to be responsible for the Garden, protecting it as a priest, a prophet, and a king. He was to sacrifice himself for his bride Eve, and he was to disclose to her all that God had instructed him, especially that which concerned the Tree of the Knowledge of Good and Evil. He was to rule over the land and treat his spouse as a queen. But what happens in this primordial story? There appears in the Garden of Eden a serpent more cunning than all of the other animals. That serpent found a way into the garden because Adam did not protect the barriers as he was instructed to do. Not only did he fail as a kingly figure by letting his guard down to evil, he also failed in protecting and laying down his life for his wife when temptation occurred. How do we know this? Because Adam is standing right next to Eve when she eats of the fruit and has a conversation with the enemy.

The story is riddled with missed opportunities, poor actions, and inadequate excuses. The conflict that occurs as a result of the Fall is very much the fault of both Adam and Eve, but instead of taking responsibility for their actions, they blame each other. "The serpent made me do it," or, "The woman you gave me made me sin"; when all along it wasn't another who made them sin. Rather, it was their own propensity toward selfishness, self-preservation, or even self-gratification that was the problem. There will always be the tendency to want to point the attention to another when we ourselves are in the line of fire for a crime of sorts.

Yet let's look to an alternative. In the New Testament we see Jesus as the Last Adam, who goes into a garden once again and takes responsibility in a way the previous Adam did not. Jesus fights to the death for his bride, holding and disclosing to all the words of the Father as a true prophet. He lays down his life as a true priest and seizes back all that the enemy stole. We can be either like Jesus, with his self-giving love for the bride, or like Adam, with his self-preserving selfishness that does nothing but blame another for his failings. Obviously the former is that to which we must strive.

It is easy to take one another for granted, to become tired of maintaining the perimeter of the garden, but we must realize that our work is not done until we are buried in the ground. I think part of the problem is that we just assume treating one another with dignity and respect will always be easy. When it is not easy at home, we must work even harder on our relationship, or the lies can grow and become more painful and divisive. Often we will afford more understanding to a stranger than our own spouse because we are not sure if the stranger is a threat or not. Or we extend the benefit of the doubt to a neighbor because conflict over the long term could be avoided by letting that offense simmer and die down. We must do even more than this in our own homes: We must strive to see the person God loves in our spouse.

For a successful marriage, we must do more than avoid a conflict or give the benefit of the doubt; we truly must make an effort at reinforcing the garden against the enemy's attempts to destroy the union God has brought together. Remember that marital Scripture, "What therefore God has joined together, let not man put asunder" (Mark 10:9)? We could easily apply that verse to this call to strengthen the foundation of our marriage with a healthy dose of dignity and respect toward our spouse. When things go wrong and difficulties arise in paradise, remember that blaming the other will never advance your cause.

The next time an argument begins, ask yourself if you have been careless in defending your spouse by allowing a serpent to cunningly creep into your midst who is leading you to look with irritation and even disdain toward your spouse. If the father of lies can whisper in our ears and provoke a blaming response in our marriages, then the wounds we can inflict on our spouses can cause even greater pain.

Activity

Ask yourself: "Are there areas where I have lessened my efforts at caring for what God has given me? How can I build up and maintain what has fallen to ruin? Have I become used to speaking poorly toward my spouse? Do I take my spouse for granted? How can I extend dignity and respect, even when my spouse doesn't behave as I would like? Have I shown disrespect for my spouse to others outside of our marriage?"

Do an inventory of the ways in which you've let your guard down in your marriage in these areas. Maybe an apology is in order for you both today.

Chapter Three

Wise Choices

The third basic quality of a solid marriage is making wise choices, which connects to the cardinal virtue of prudence. This is not about just picking something good over something bad; rather, it is making a choice that will enable you to become the saint you are called to be. In marriage, we need prudence to guide our choices.

Linda

The truth is that the end result of our life will be determined by all of the small choices we make along the way. So the question is: What end result do you want? Do you want a marriage in which you still enjoy being together and have common interests that are beyond raising your children? Do you want to experience the blessing of deep trusting love that brings a host of peace and joy? Do you want your children to be walking in the faith that you have given them? These things don't just happen by coincidence. It takes hard work and wise choices along the way to find yourself in a place of contentment in your twilight years.

As married people, our choices no longer affect just us. In both the big decisions and the small ones, the way we choose to act, the things we place at the forefront of our priorities, and the way we live our lives leave a lasting impression on those around us, especially our spouse and children.

Life is filled with choices. What job should I take? Which house should we buy? Should we move or should we stay? Is it time to have another child? Can we afford to buy a new dishwasher or should we continue suffering with hand washing? As Chris and I have aged, we have found that basic life decisions become more difficult. I think that's because we have more to lose. It was easier moving the family when the kids were young. Yet once they put down roots and get involved in school activities and specific courses of study, moving requires more certainty. Financial decisions require more caution because there is less time in our future to make up for large mistakes. Transferring jobs gets tricky, and we get set in our ways, making us more leery of change. But through it all, the best way to weather the storms of both good and bad decisions is to make the choices together.

I view life as an adventure. I don't want to live a life where I am filled with regret at the end of it because I was afraid to follow my dreams and desires. Chris and I have always judged a choice by two main criteria. The most important consideration is to make sure what we are contemplating is not in opposition to the clear will of God. Is it something we know would be morally wrong? If so, then it can't even be an option. The second consideration is to determine how this choice lines up with our ultimate desires and dreams. We have found that God usually leads us by our desires. "Take delight in the Lord, and he will give you the desires of your heart" (Psalm 37:4). As long as we are pliable and open to whichever direction the Lord will lead, we usually steer toward the choice we want most. We have found that God is big enough to keep us from making really bad choices if we have sought him humbly and honestly through the process.

A couple of years into our marriage, I was teaching full time in a public school. Despite the fact that we already had one child at the time, I had agreed to do this so Chris could finish his bachelor's degree. Once he was finished, I wanted to quit. For me, the greatest desire of my heart was to be at home with my kids, and I didn't want to spend my days away from them if I didn't have to. Well, it happened to work out that at the exact time that I was gearing up to leave the workforce to be a stay-at-home mom, Chris felt called to go into full-time ministry. Now we were faced with the choice of either both of us being without jobs or just one of us quitting a job. I knew his heart's desire to serve God full time, and he knew the ache in my heart to be home with our babies. In the end, I quit my job and Chris pursued full-time ministry. Yes, everyone thought we were crazy. We walked away from salaries and benefits to follow both of our hearts.

It took years for us to get to the point financially where we were not nearly drowning each month. We found groceries left on our porch by generous donors, and we faithfully prayed for money to show up in the mail during difficult months. There were times of great stress and panic. However, through it all, we never doubted our choice to pursue what we loved. We were both doing what we wanted and what we felt led by God to be doing. I didn't have to experience resentment toward Chris because he followed his dream and vise versa. And because we made this decision together, we couldn't blame each other during the tough times. To this day, I am so grateful for the grace we were given to take that leap of faith. Our life has never stopped being miraculous, and we have never regretted that decision made so long ago.

Making basic life decisions together, seeking the desires and needs of both spouses, is a sure way to reach an end result that gives joy. Yet, the choices we make regarding our own spiritual lives and the spiritual growth of our spouse and children hold an even more weighty responsibility. Honestly, there is nothing more important in my life than the spiritual well-being of my husband and children. I feel that I will have failed in my main job on this earth if I lose one of them to the enemy's lies.

I am fully aware that, as our children grow, they will choose their own path and get the wonderful privilege of making their own mistakes. Some of our kids will fight every attempt we make to encourage them to walk in the faith, but we must have hope that God will not ignore our efforts or the tear-stained pillows where many prayers are prayed. "Train up a child in the way he should go, and when he is old he will not depart from it" (Proverbs 22:6). These inspired words give me much comfort and hope that God is more than capable of making up for all of the mistakes I have made in trying to share my faith with my children. Yet I must keep trying.

Chris and I are pretty messed-up individuals. There are definitely days when the only thing we are absolutely sure about is our own incompetence! But we thank God for the grace he generously pours into our lives. Furthermore, I am eternally grateful for the spiritual leadership of my husband. For as long as I have known Chris, he has desired to lead me (and our family) to Christ. In fact, this was one of the qualities that attracted me to him in the first place. Chris is aware of his own weaknesses and his need for Christ's mercy and grace. And it's through that humility that he leads our family. He lives his need for Jesus openly before us, and we all desire to live that kind of faith.

One of his favorite sacraments is reconciliation. If it were left up to me, our family would go to confession probably only a couple of times a year, usually when the Church strongly encourages it. However, Chris is a strong believer in frequent confession. He has the priest on speed dial! He's the one who rallies the troops on Saturday afternoon and drives us to church so we can stand in line for an hour waiting our turn. Sure, my kids whine and complain sometimes, but they have learned it is futile. Their dad has made the wise choice that frequenting the sacrament of reconciliation is a priority in our family. What a gift! This choice has already reaped beautiful benefits for our children. Our oldest children now choose to regularly attend confession, even without our encouragement. During their own struggles, they have found amazing grace in that sacrament. Even as teenagers, they manage to find an hour on a busy Saturday afternoon to stand in line without any of us. To me, this is a miracle. But in reality, it's simply the grace of God working in our children's lives because their father made the wise choice to make his faith a priority.

It is true that our salvation is an unmerited gift from Jesus. There is nothing we can do to earn it. It is also true that people who have grown up in completely faithless homes have found the mercy of God through salvation. However, as spouses and parents, we cannot leave such an important part of our family's lives to chance. We must make choices that will positively impact their hearts, steering them toward Christ. Of course, it must always begin in our own hearts. We must set ourselves right with God and work to find perfection on our own spiritual journeys. After we are heading down the right path, though, we must be sure to make the correct decisions for those we love.

Wise choices will determine our end result. Making smart choices together will ensure not only one's marital union, but will impact one's family in a profound way. "As a result, with their parents leading the way by example and family prayer, children and indeed everyone gathered around the family hearth will find a readier path to human maturity, salvation, and holiness."[3]

Chris

Just as many golfers appreciate another chance, I think most of us would wish for a mulligan when it comes to many of our earlier choices. If we had known then what we know now, it would be a whole new round. It takes a special person to learn from the mistakes of others—and possibly an exceptionally intelligent and perceptive individual to learn from one's own earlier mistakes.

I remember hearing a priest give the definition of insanity as repeatedly doing the same thing, thinking it would yield different results. I suppose we are all a little insane. A few of you reading this book may be the exception to the rule and have spent most of your life avoiding the pitfalls of others and learning from each of your failures. Well, here's a simple tell-tale way to see if that's truly the case: How many times do you go to reconciliation and confess the same sins? Okay, now that we are all on the same playing field, we can move on!

Making wise choices is not impossible, but it certainly isn't as easy as simply knowing the right answer and putting it into play at the appropriate time. We undeniably want to do this, but the struggle to do so is experienced by us all. Let's connect this attribute for a successful marriage to the cardinal virtue of prudence. Making wise choices is imperative for a successful marriage, but this is a quality that must grow and develop, like working out particular muscles for a specific sport.

I remember trying out for the wrestling team when I was a child. This is one of those things I wish I had thought through a bit more before jumping into the singlet! First, in order for me to have a chance at success, I had to drop an insane amount of weight because I would need to wrestle a kid who was about four years old in order to have a chance at winning a match. Second, I had never "worked out" in the weight room in any serious way before, which apparently was necessary for me to be successful. So, to improve and have a shot at getting through a match without hurling all over a hapless victim, I went into the gym at the break of dawn to lift weights. I must have felt like I was invincible or that this whole pumping iron thing was pretty easy because I really pushed the limits. As the day progressed, I began to feel sore, and by the time I took my shower, I could barely lift my arms to my head in order to apply the shampoo. I basically had ripped every muscle in my body and couldn't move. I felt intense pain, and as I wandered around the school the following days, I wondered if I really wanted to be a wrestler in the first place.

One of the gifts of marriage is that both spouses bring a wealth of life experiences into the decision-making process, and hopefully together a couple can avoid making mistakes that they'll regret. Here is one thing I know about Linda: She is a lot more rational and smart about everything than I am. So when it comes to wise choices, I listen very carefully to her. I am confident that if she were with me that day long ago when I stumbled into the weight room, she would have told me to relax and pace myself. I would have ignored her—but would have admitted later that she was right.

Let's look at the false perspective concerning wise choices, and then explore a new way of thinking.

False Perspective

What benefits me individually? This is, right out of the gate, a false perspective.

In marriage, we are no longer making decisions that impact only our individual selves. When you as a couple approach any number of choices—finances, family commitments, basic employment options, home locations, and so on—one of you cannot simply ask how it will make you feel. Making choices cannot be done on an individual basis within a marriage, nor can this be reduced down to a "feeling."

Here are a few basic problems with the "feeling" approach to choices: First, your feelings fluctuate on a regular basis. It may have to do with lack of sleep, the food you've eaten, or the constant worrying about something you can't control, but in the end, you cannot make a responsible decision based on feelings that change. Second, your understanding of the choice to be made must be explored. Rarely do we just know perfectly, from some unseen word of knowledge, what it is that we must do in a particular scenario. In marriage, you must address the choice with your spouse in mind, and if you have children, considering your decision's impact upon the kids is paramount. It is a false premise to conclude that as a couple you will approach every decision the same—or that you will feel exactly in sync about the route you decide upon. It is a false premise that you will always just know what to do, or that you will both have a feeling that makes sense. I would guess that most would agree with this, and yet how often do we make decisions like that?

I remember when Linda and I were living in West Palm Beach and a new Bally Total Fitness opened, with all its fancy treadmills and weight machines. (At this point I'm guessing you're asking: When will he learn?) So, my wife and I sat and listened to the pitch, having toured the facility with the wonderfully in-shape salespeople. I often imagine I look better than I do, but occasionally I have moments when I decide I must get more in shape and be healthier and realize I'm not doing anything about it at home. So, if I want to really change, I must go somewhere—like a gym. While the finances of a regular commitment would be a stretch for us, we both thought this was a good choice. Just so you know, it wasn't. First, the gym was not near our home, and second, I didn't like working out! But I was in a contract and couldn't just get out of it. Finally, due to a move we made, I was able to sever my ties with that establishment, but joining that gym was not a wise decision.

Marriage is filled with these kinds of live-and-learn scenarios, as evidenced by the story of our first car lease. Linda felt warning signals the moment we walked into the Mitsubishi dealership, but I was just plain sick of owning crappy cars. We hastily went for it, and it was all wrong. The Galant lease is an example of a horrible, impulsive choice that has had a lasting negative impact. The experience gave birth to our "Whatever we do, let's not have another Mitsubishi Galant situation" warning. I will say here and now, Linda was right, and I was wrong. I didn't realize something early in marriage that I am now fully aware of: Making wise decisions is not easy, nor should it be done without prayerful and careful analysis. I needed a new way of thinking.

A New Way of Thinking

Discerning what benefits each individual and the family as a whole is key in every decision. This marital theme of wise choices connects to prudence because it is about pursuing the avenue that will help us and our families become the saints we are called to be. In a marriage, we must ask how the choices we make will enhance and provide a better path toward marital and family sanctity. What we choose as a family will impact one another individually, but also others collectively. And placing our choices in God's hands brings about the miracles we need. The choice to be open to life, to entrust our finances to God, and to be balanced instead of extreme are all relevant. How can we make wise choices?

First, ask what your spouse feels about a particular choice. When Linda was hesitant about signing the lease, I should have left the car dealership immediately. My problem is that I tend to feel a sense of obligation to buy something after a salesperson spends a long time showing me a particular product. I know—I am my own worst enemy. If I would have listened to Linda's hesitancy alone, I would have avoided years of agony, and by years I mean many *years*.

Second, ask what impact a choice will have upon your family. If I have an obsession with buying a Volkswagen Beetle (which by the way I love) and attempt to buy one (which by the way I have not), that would be insane since I have nine kids! Clowns spilling out of a car at the circus is cute, but Padgetts falling out of a Beetle is just plain wrong.

Third, we can look at the Scriptures, which are filled with real-life stories about people who have failed and succeeded in their faith life. We can also read the documents of the Church about particular matters, and we can spend time reading about the lives of saints who attempted to live the faith in their particular day and age.

When you compare your own feelings to the input of spouse, family, Scripture, Church, and saints, those feelings should either be in sync with the rest or jettisoned from the process. Are there times when you make a decision contrary to Scripture or the Catholic Church? I suppose those will be the times you regret. Are there times when you make a decision in opposition to your wife? Only if you are an idiot.

One final word about the role of faith in decision making. I've always been baffled by people who let their kids make their own choices about whether to attend Mass or not. Really? Do you let your kids choose whether or not to go to school? No! Why not? Because they have to get an education or they won't be able to function in society in a contributing way, let alone have the chance to get a decent job or go on to college. Most kids, if left to their own devices, would probably stay home and play Minecraft all day long. Why is it that, with all of the choices we make as a family regarding sports, music lessons, education, and vacations, the faith life is often the one area that is expendable? For a marriage to not only function but thrive, you must make the choice to put your faith at the top of your list of priorities. That choice alone will have the most eternal of consequences.

Activity

Ask yourself: "What are the priorities in our marriage and family? What choices can we change? What if we add one thing or take one other thing away? How will that action impact our marriage?"

Write down what you do for the week, and discuss together if this is what you want to be doing next year.

Chapter Four

Commitment

The fourth basic quality of a solid marriage is commitment. This attribute connects to the cardinal virtue of fortitude—a willingness to hold fast to the truth even to the point of death. We need fortitude in marriage, and it is previewed with the vow: "Till death do us part."

Linda

Everything in life that is worth doing takes commitment to get it done. Most of us know that achieving success at work, running a marathon, getting healthy, or finishing school requires more than just a passive decision to complete. Yet some fail to understand that marriage requires a lot more commitment than any of these. Why? Because marriage is a lifetime commitment, and it involves another party that can sometimes make it difficult to stay committed! Making a resolve toward commitment is crucial, and it must be a commitment to both God and each other.

I truly believe it is a miracle when a marriage survives when God has not been present in it. When trouble hits, there needs to be something stronger than just the two individuals to carry them through. Therefore, commitment to God, both personally and collectively, needs to be established from the beginning. The best thing Chris and I did for our marriage happened while we were dating. For a couple of years before our nuptials, we realigned our relationship, put Christ at the center, and focused on our own personal walk with God. The lesson we learned was that a strong spiritual bond in marriage can only be attained when each individual has his or her own relationship with Christ. I found that during difficult times in our lives, my saving grace was my trust in God and my desire to serve him fully. When my faith is correctly placed, I can allow those difficulties to work themselves out.

I am blessed to have a husband who has always lived out his responsibility to be a spiritual leader in our family. However, because life is a series of different seasons and hills and valleys, there have been times in our marriage when one or the other have gotten sloppy in our pursuit of God. Other priorities have come in and distracted us, or we simply got burned out. Yet almost always, when one of us is down, the other takes the reins. The fact that both of us have our own individual relationships with Christ makes this possible.

Years ago, when Chris was traveling with his band, he would come home completely exhausted. He still is exhausted these days when he arrives home, but in those days, the band traveled solely by van. That meant hours and hours of traffic and late-night driving. Combine that with the physical exertion of a live concert to hundreds of teens, and Chris would be almost useless when he got home. There were many Sunday mornings when I would be ready to leave for church and he would be debating about getting out of bed at all. Those were the days when we were not Catholic, and the incentive to attend services on Sunday was not as strong, especially after he had just spent days at church-related events. As he would lie in bed, I would gently inform him that if he were not going to church with me, I was going to leave the small, crazy children home with him. He was almost always dressed in a matter of minutes! But truly, even though he was worn out, he knew that his place was with his family, worshipping God together.

This kind of encouragement has gone both ways. As I mentioned, Chris is the one who reminds me of the importance of the sacrament of reconciliation, as he gently motivates our family to seek grace there. In fact, the reason our family converted to the Catholic Church in the first place was because of Chris's driving desire to seek Christ and fully understand his teachings. My confidence in his desire to please God allowed me to trust his leadership, especially as we entered the unknown world of Catholicism.

Our personal commitment to God not only reaps benefits for our spouses, it also provides a lasting foundation for the future faith of our children. I am convinced—*completely* convinced—that I am walking with God today because of the commitment my mom made to Jesus. After years of not being able to have children, she knew when God granted her that privilege it came with the heavy responsibility of raising her children to know God. Though she was not trained in great theological studies nor gifted with an ability to communicate the beautiful truths of our faith clearly, she did all she could to lead her children to Christ. Despite the lack of support from my dad and our childish complaints, every Sunday morning she would say, "By golly, we will go to church on Sunday." There was no room for discussion or debate. Her simple commitment to getting her daughters to church has left the lasting mark of faith in all of our lives. Today, all three of us girls walk with God and are training our children to do so, as well. What a great legacy!

My mom's stubborn commitment was passed down to me. In the early years of my motherhood, when Chris was traveling doing ministry, I still knew I had to train my children in our faith. With little babies and toddlers on hand, I would muster all the strength I had to drag my herd of children to church. I knew that any excuses I could think of ("I'm too tired. I just stand in the back anyway. I can't hear the readings. I'm distracting others") were not good enough. I did not want to stand before God on judgment day and hope those flimsy excuses would be enough to get me to heaven. By golly, we go to church on Sunday!

To pass our faith on to our children, we must posses it ourselves first. To have a marriage in which Christ is the center and grace radiates out from that center, there needs to be a personal commitment to Christ first. Start there, with your own heart.

Now, of course, commitment to God is not the only focus necessary in a marriage. It may seem obvious, but it needs to be mentioned that commitment to each other is also fundamental. Every couple needs to have a stubborn, unspoken declaration to each other that no matter what comes against them, "You shall not pass!" Just picture Gandalf lifting that glowing staff in the air and declaring with deep certainty that he will not allow anything, no matter how scary and powerful, to get past him and cause harm to those in his care. *That* is the kind of commitment necessary to guard your marriage against all the dangers that desire to cause harm.

The dangers in a marriage don't usually present themselves as fiery beasts from the pits of hell, but they are just as evil. Sometimes those dangers resemble a coworker who has a way of flirting a little too much or a loving mother who voices her disapproval of your spouse too often. Other times, those dangers can take the form of financial success that draws you away from the family or personal failures that send you into a hole of self-loathing that barricades you from the ones who can help the most. Then, of course, those dangers can be as simple and ugly as selfishness and pride, when the most important person in this marriage is...me.

Even though Chris and I have a really good marriage, it is far from perfect. Over the years, we have seen dangers come into the mix that could easily have threatened the trust and safety we have in each other. During those difficult times, it certainly was not our warm, fuzzy, romantic, emotional love that kept us together. It was simply our commitment. In any marriage, there come times when emotions and feelings have to be placed to the side and logic and reasoning need to take over. Times when you need to remind yourself that this commitment you made to your spouse goes deeper than the surface of feelings, deeper than your wants and desires, deeper than your very needs and rights. There may be times in your marriage when your commitment to your spouse cuts deeper than anything involving yourself and rests solely on the strength of God. It may not be pretty or what you signed up for on the day of your dream wedding, but that's commitment, and sometimes it hurts.

Finally, if large beasts do threaten your marriage and strain your commitment, it is important to find good, godly counsel. Put aside pride and seek the prayers and support of those you trust. In many cases, having a chance to just talk openly and expose the secret darkness helps to start the journey toward healing and renewal.

Chris

Many years ago, I was sitting with my good friend Bob in his boat on a lake in Iowa. We were talking about the need to see marriages flourish and the problems many relationships seem to suffer from. We were talking about the crisis in the Church with all of the priest scandals; we were dreaming about possible talks we would do together—in other words, we were solving all of the world's problems while floating around. Bob said, "We talk about a crisis in the priesthood now, but what if half of our priests also left their vocations to go and do something else? Now, *that* would be a crisis. But that abandonment of one's vocation is happening in marriages right now." I will forever try to claim that insight as my own, but you've seen the truth! Bob Perron is a genius.

This *is* the crisis in marriage we are now facing. Really, it is no wonder there is such popularity in shows dealing with supposed bachelors trying to find true love. We love the drama, and in some small way, the populace wants to see people implode right before their eyes. From their ratings, these relational conflicts seem to be fun to watch, but nobody ever wants their own dating relationships or marriages to collapse. Unfortunately, the mockery of authentic marriages is ever before us in the media, and too many people have a firsthand account of what it was like to see the dysfunction in their family's marriages growing up. Is there really a hope of doing something different in our marriages that our culture, media, and even family heritage haven't been able to achieve? Can we have marriages that last, or, even more radical, can we have marriages that thrive? I am certain that we can!

I remember visiting my grandparents in a suburb of Detroit when I was four years old. The family gathered annually at their home in Birmingham, Michigan, where there always was great celebrations, laughter, games of spin the bottle and pool, and quite a lot of drinking. I was almost one month away from my fifth birthday, and I remember my father taking me into the living room to have a serious conversation. It may have been the only time during the holiday that I wasn't completely jacked up on Faygo, the sugary soda that in all honesty was liquid heaven for a child one sip away from chronic hyperactivity. He told me that when I got home from vacation, he wouldn't be there anymore. He was no longer going to be living in the same house with my mother, my sister, and me. I really had no idea what he was talking about. In fact, all I wanted to do was focus my attention deficit disorder on the walkie-talkie and candy I'd gotten for Christmas. I don't remember much more about the holiday, but when my mother, my sister, and I walked up to our back door in Valley City, North Dakota, I was surprised to see the door open from the inside and my father's face come into view. I said with childhood sensitivity and tact: "I thought you weren't going to be here when I got home."

We entered the warm house, and life continued along for me as if nothing had ever been said in Michigan. I'm not sure when the official divorce took place, but one day my dad was living at the other end of town, and this time it was without any specific word to prepare me. Every weekend, my sister and I would leave my mother and go spend time with my dad and his lady friend. From the beginning, I knew that my mother was not pleased with this woman. While I was not privy to the reasons for her animosity, I embraced my mother's feelings of irritation and anger toward this intruder and made them my own. I felt very awkward about her role in my life, and I even recall penning a specific note to her that simply stated: "I hate you." I was a minimalist writer, much like Hemingway, when I was young. She was obviously hurt by my comment, and I could read the pain in her eyes.

Being a sensitive boy, I tried to remedy my mistake by writing "I love you." I didn't mean it, but I wanted to try to bring about a resolution so that she would not be so sad. She told me that she understood why I wrote the second note, in order to try to make amends for the first, but what she really wanted was for my words to be filled with sincerity. I knew that affection for her could never happen. I didn't love my father's girlfriend and eventual wife. All I wanted was for my parents to find a way to start anew. Couldn't they at least try to fix their marriage? Even though I was young, and without deep theological and religious training, I knew that the separation of my parents was not the way things were supposed to be. I wanted my dad around, and deep down I wanted him to love my mother. Over time, I grew to love my father's wife, but a child's hurt is not something to gloss over, and it wasn't easy for me to forget.

Over the years, I would try to trick my parents into getting back together again. I'd ask my mother if she would be open to reconciling with my father, and she often replied that she would be open to this, but certain things would have to change. I would assume the stipulation might have been the ousting of the woman my father was living with. When an ideal opportunity would arise, I would ask my father if he would consider getting back together with my mother, but he always told me that, while he loved my sister and me, he certainly didn't have the same feelings toward my mother that he used to have. He would convey that the two of them had gone off in two different directions, and, while my mother was willing to change paths and accompany him on his, he was not interested in her as a companion any longer.

I was crestfallen. There was really nothing I could do to fix the marriage. I did pray an awful lot for the two to be reconciled, but it seemed that my requests bounced from the ceiling and back onto the bed, bounding away without resolution. Over the years I would get on planes or buses with my sister in order to go visit my father, who had moved to a different state. The heartache of leaving my mother for extended periods of time would be duplicated when I'd have to leave my father weeks later in order to return home. We were torn between two worlds, and while it made Christmas fun—getting all those extra presents—I would have traded anything to have had a "normal" family again.

My parents' divorce was final. My father was very faithful to remind us of how much he loved us, and he called every Saturday to check in on my sister and me. But there was no hope of a miracle in sight, and as a result, there were many things I began to embrace about masculinity and relationships that would impact my perspective of God, family, personhood, and marriage. I am confident that my father would have done anything he could have to negate the suffering his children felt as a result of the divorce. He labored to this end, often asking how we felt and giving us permission to be blunt in processing it all, and for that I am thankful.

As I have grown into a man of faith, my constant phrase has been: I serve a God of new beginnings! When all is said and done, although it's likely that half of us have come from broken homes and would have loved to have had a family that was less dysfunctional, in the end we have a chance to implement the positive things we have seen and completely change the negative.

In the sacrament of marriage, we really are enabled by the Spirit of God to truly love in a way that is life-giving. I am hopeful that even if you find yourself in a situation such as my own, you will realize that all is not lost. While things will be more challenging in our application of love and marital intimacy, we can truly find ourselves in a holy place with our spouse that will not only bring us into the arms of Jesus, but will also leave a living legacy of relational integrity to our children. Marriages are in crisis, but our God of new beginnings is inviting us to really press in to the richness of his presence in our lives.

What I longed for with my parents and what I hope for in my own marriage is the attribute of commitment that I tie to the cardinal virtue of fortitude. When we think of the virtue of fortitude, it is more than just a tenacious and steadfast commitment to something because it is important. This is a good quality to have, but fortitude is more than being determined; rather, within the Christian context, it is a willingness to both live and even die for the faith. We need this type of commitment in marriages for them to last.

When a couple says that divorce is not an option, which is what I had determined for my own marriage in the light of my parents' marital unraveling, it's a step in the right direction. What makes a person stay committed "until death do us part" is certainly not just attraction, or common interests, or even passion. We are all going to sag and get old and wrinkled, and, while there will be times of passion as we get older, staying together with someone for decade after decade has to be more than just physical. Having common interests are important, too, but you will grow in a number of ways, with interests differing one from another.

False Perspective

One false perspective is that commitment is of value when it benefits my dreams, my agenda, and my life. Another false perspective is that, while commitment is valuable, there are also reasons not to be committed, and my inconvenience or fears will determine my course of action. And still another is that commitment will be natural or even easy. I think anyone who has been married for longer than the initial honeymoon phase knows that isn't the case. You can't just accidentally be committed to your spouse, nor can you think it will be a natural result of the two becoming one. We need a new way of thinking.

A New Way of Thinking

A holy marriage is a witness of God's love for the world, Christ's love for the Church, and can change society. In other words, marriage is commitment because it is beyond passion, common interests, compatibility, and convenience; and this is because marriage is holy in its reflection of God in time. The impact and reasons for commitment are tied to the responsibility and desire for imitation that others will have upon witnessing a marriage grounded in fortitude. Fortitude is needed for the marital impact to remain, enduring the most difficult of times because the union is worthy of such a battle. If you were to look at key military battles over the course of history, some would seem impossible to commit to because of the grand potential of one's loss of life. And yet some surges that seemed doomed to fail from the start were of the utmost necessity nonetheless. Is your marriage worth fighting for? Is your spouse worth dying for? This is why marriage prep is so important—because the cost and necessity for success are so great.

Marriage is such a holy responsibility, and your spouse is worth an entire commitment, just as Jesus Christ gave a total commitment toward his Church. Mary was also committed to the mission of her Son. Her trust and belief helped to bring about the miracle others received. You and your spouse are one flesh. It is time to put an emphasis on commitment toward one another in marriage and together toward God.

Activity

Ask yourself: "Are there any beasts working to tear down my marriage? Threats trying to undermine the work of God in the unity between us? How will my commitment—or lack thereof—impact our children? Is my commitment with God where it should be?"

If it is possible to find the initial vows you spoke to one another on your wedding day, it would be beautiful to renew them one evening together. Your willingness and purposeful pursuing of the depth of marriage is something that can encourage your commitment to each other and to God.

Chapter Five

Self-Control

The fifth basic quality of a solid marriage is self-control. This attribute is connected to the cardinal virtue of temperance, which we need to control our various appetites. It is a virtue sorely needed in a day and age where self-gratification is heralded.

Linda

Marriage would be easy if both of us were perfect. I would even imagine that my life in general would be pretty amazing if I could polish up that one virtue of self-control. If I had an ironclad will and optimal self-control, I would probably be skinnier, healthier, more financially stable, smarter, and the best wife in the world. But alas, I am human, and virtue is a lot more difficult to attain than just by wishing it here.

If you have been married for more than one day, you have realized that marriage is filled with situations that require self-control—temptation is always around the corner. Temptation does not just take the form of a good-looking man or a pretty woman. It can also look like the urge to lie to or verbally assault your spouse. It can take the shape of a beautiful glazed donut or an extra glass of wine. Temptation can look like the newest electronic device or the desire to not get your work done that day. Whatever the form, there are two things necessary to overcome temptation and to increase self-control.

The first important point to remember is that self-control requires you to *keep your eye on the prize*. "Don't sacrifice what you ultimately want for what you want in the moment." This anonymous quote has gotten me through many temptations. I ask myself, "What do I ultimately want?" I want a happy marriage. I want to be healthy. I want my husband and children to be saints. I want to be holy. When my eye is on those prizes, I find that self-control is easier to acquire.

One day, Chris and I had a heated disagreement. Yes, those do happen in our household. It must not have been a major issue because I can't seem to remember the cause of it—but I do recall that we both felt confident that we were right. Eventually things cooled off, and as the day went on, we both decided to just move on past the conflict. We were back to living our happy, crazy existence until that evening. As we sat relaxing in the brief quiet of a childless room, something happened that clearly proved that I was right all along in our earlier disagreement. I clearly remember the choice that lay before me in that instant. That quote flashed before my eyes, and the voice of God spoke to my heart. He said, "Linda, what do you ultimately want? Do you want a peaceful marriage, or do you want to be right?" Oh boy, I wanted to be right! I wanted to inform Chris all about how wrong he was, but my eye was on the prize. I kept my mouth shut, and we continued our wonderful, peaceful evening.

This idea of keeping your eye on the prize, that ultimate goal in your life, can be applied to any number of situations you encounter in marriage or on your own personal journey. I have used it repeatedly in my attempts to get healthy. For me, saying no to a warm, gooey brownie is not simple, but when I remember my ultimate goal, I find the strength to walk away. On a larger scale, I have been able to find the strength needed to persevere in difficult situations, like homeschooling my children, because I know what I ultimately want to see at the end of the journey.

What is your ultimate goal in your marriage? How do the choices you make, both personally and collectively, impact that goal? Even though communicating our feelings is important to a healthy relationship, a constant war to be right or "obeyed" is only going to cause more frustration and conflict. Even those seemingly small situations when we fail to use self-control can build up to large issues. That next glass of wine, those amazing deals on sale, that little lie, or that extra hour of sleep that prevents you from going to Mass can all grow into larger and larger issues if they are not kept in check with self-control. Keep your eye on the prize.

The second point to remember in our pursuit of self-control is that *balance is the key*. I have a saying that I have tried to work into my life for years: "Extremes are easy; balance is difficult." I believe that the only extreme that God calls us to is to love others—we can never love a person too much. However, in life overall, we are called to walk a balanced existence. The call to be in the world, but not of it, is an assignment that cannot be attained without balance.

In our family we have battled with many choices in the attempt to find our path toward holiness. The questions of owning a TV or not, our girls wearing pants or not, allowing rock music or not (and the list can go on) have caused us to flip-flop many times in trying to find the place where we fit. In the end, we have decided that our image of a good family and marriage will be unique and different from that of everyone else. We've had to find what works for us, and for us it is all about balance. It's perfectly fine if a couple decides to eliminate the influence of television or secular music from their family, but we find we are consistently called back to my saying: "Extremes are easy; balance is difficult." It is a lot easier to control what your children watch on TV if you don't own one, but balancing their exposure requires the development of self-control and discipline. It's a lot easier to dress modestly if you shop for dresses at the local Amish clothing store, but learning to present yourself in a modest way actually using the fashion of the day requires a lot more self-control and work.

When I was in college, I went through a fashion stage that we refer to as "the holiness dress" phase. I wore unflattering dresses to my ankle and no makeup. This was a huge change for me, for, growing up in Florida, I was always a shorts-and-tee-shirt kind of girl. The reason for my change of attire was the desire to be more modest and holy for Chris, my boyfriend at the time. Obviously my motivation was right, but the extremes to which I took it ultimately made me stressed and unhappy. I thought I was doing the right thing, but I felt trapped in that extreme, unable to fully be myself. Thankfully, this phase did not last too long. I eventually learned that modesty could be acquired by less extreme measures. I just needed to find the balance between being myself and being respectful to the goal of chastity.

Through our marriage, there have been several times when we made choices that were ultimately too extreme for us. In those situations, we were usually following the example or advice of someone else instead of seeking what was best for us personally. Those extremes never lasted long because we ended up cracking, unable to maintain that high standard. Peace and joy in our household was restored only when our balance was found. The main problem with extremes is that they often force you to become someone that you are not. Improving in virtue is necessary, but natural growth that is accompanied by little stretches once in a while tends to be solidified as a permanent part of one's character. When we force ourselves and our loved ones into extremes, conflict can easily arise. We must be ourselves and allow our spouses to be who they are—and then pursue holiness together.

Self-control is a virtue we must learn to perfect, but we must not strive for that perfection by pursuing extremes. We cannot eliminate temptation from our lives, so we must learn to choose correctly when it comes along. If we have hidden ourselves away, we will never learn the balance that is required to obtain self-control.

Ultimately I want to live a full, happy life alongside a man who is joining me in the pursuit of holiness. I want us to raise our children to walk in that same faith. Therefore, the choices

I make must reflect the virtue of self-control. I cannot allow bad behavior, immoral choices, and unruly thoughts to lead me down a path that takes me away from my goals. I must also find that balance in the way I live that gives me the freedom to be myself, free from the bondage of extremes, while pursuing those goals in self-control. This is a difficult pursuit. Perfection would make it a lot simpler. If only I were perfect!

Chris

I am certain that you can think of countless examples when a particular spouse has little self-control, and unfortunately the ramifications cause the family unit to break down. It is common for people to think of the sin of lust when it comes to a lack of self-control, and while this is certainly applicable, I am speaking far more broadly. For example, it's necessary to have self-control when it comes to finances, dealing with discipline, and addressing any of the variables attached to deadly sins like wrath, greed, envy, and pride. Self-control is key in marital success.

I have a friend who has had a very difficult marriage. Her husband has been unfaithful numerous times, and it seems that even with all of the information about the ramifications of the acts of infidelity and lust, he still struggles to stay faithful. What I realized over the years of interacting with this couple is that it would be easy for any number of us to fall into such difficulties, and while many might insist that isn't the case for them, I would argue we are all prone to self-destructive tendencies in some area.

We are all sinful, broken, and weak—and are all in need of a Savior. The problem with sin is that, once entered into, it opens the door to even more aspects of compromise. Sin is a gateway drug, if you will, for even more uncharitable behavior—sin leads to more sin. What often happens is that small steps in sin eventually take a person to the precipice, and if the habitual tendency to give in to that sin occurs one time too many, a fatal consequence occurs. Rarely is it the case that someone wakes up and determines to lose his home while gambling that evening, or decides that this very day will be the day she chooses to commit adultery. It is small acts that gain momentum until they take on a mind of their own. What are the false perspectives people have about self-control?

False Perspective

Many people see self-control as something important for public behavior, sports, and business, but they think that, when it comes to marriage, it should be natural. For example, there is a common mindset that once a person gets married, he or she will no longer struggle with lustful thoughts and actions because now sexual experiences are available with that person's spouse.

Just as athletes must discipline themselves in order to attain the prize of excellence, so too must couples discipline themselves so they can achieve long-lasting and healthy marriages. We need a new and proper perspective about marriage, and the virtue of temperance will assist us in doing just that.

A New Way of Thinking

Marriage will need to practice self-denial/self-sacrifice instead of self-gratification if it is going to blossom into something beautiful. Jesus Christ is our model of what it means to be fully human, and his life is abundant with generous moments of self-sacrifice. Think of the moment in the Garden where he prays to the Father not for his will to be done but for his Father's.

The cardinal virtue of temperance helps us to harness the passions we have within us due to concupiscence. We need to grow in temperance because our natural inclination may be to do what makes us feel good and not what makes us live in a manner befitting a child of God. Controlling our appetites is an ongoing yes to the Spirit of God within us, and it is possible not to gratify the desires of our sinful nature by walking in that same Spirit (see Galatians 5:16). We understand the virtue of not giving in to every desire in sports or at the workplace, or even within societal ethics, but somehow we minimize the importance of this in marriage. I can't say whatever comes to my mind when I am irritated in the workplace, nor can I drive over the neighborhood kid walking slowly in front of my car even if that were my greatest desire at the moment. I can't expect to win the big game if I don't spend time conditioning my body and learning all the plays, nor can I think I should be able to take something that appeals to me even if it isn't mine. Self-control is a daily part of our lives, and it has been developed in certain areas of our life to the point where we may not even think of it. If our formation as children taught us that lying, stealing, and cheating were not acceptable, over the years it often becomes second nature to purchase instead of take what we want.

I remember hearing a story from a priest in New Zealand who had a great love for meat pies. He had decided not to eat them in order to avoid too many calories and save some money, but his habit was not so easily broken. The priest told how his demise usually started with a thought. He remembered that the pie shop was putting up a new sign, and he decided to just drive by the shop and see what the finished sign looked like. Then, after seeing the sign, he noticed that one of the new pies being offered was a particular kind he had never had before, so he decided to go into the store and just look at the pie. He was still not going to eat it; after all, he had decided to not give in to that temptation. When he went into the store, the smells were overwhelming, and he looked longingly at the pie, deciding to take a tiny taste. After all, a tiny taste wasn't the same thing as buying and eating a whole slice. Plus, if he took a tiny taste, he may not like it at all, and this could just quench the desire all at once. Of course, you know what happened. Not only did he like the taste, he loved it—and bought the whole pie.

This is probably one of the best examples of the way temptation works. It's the same as an alcoholic taking a route home that would cause him to walk right past his old bar. These are called occasions of sin, and often we lose our battle with self-control even before we ready our defenses because we set ourselves up for failure. We need to have a plan of action and put our bodies into submission to our will. But this is something that doesn't accidentally happen; rather, we need to implore the Spirit of God for help.

Let's take a step back and look at a couple of basics. First, because of original sin, we are all born without original justice and are in need of God's saving grace. At baptism we are born again, filled with grace so that we can be the men and women we are called to be. The idea that being human is to act upon every desire we have is insane. And just because we are baptized doesn't mean that we now have complete and total self-control in every scenario we face. Because of the ramifications of sin, even post-baptism we have a propensity for sin that can easily be fanned into flame. This inclination is concupiscence. The good news is that we don't have to give in to every passion we experience. We all have passions, and some are ordered while others are disordered. It is fine to give in to an ordered passion: a passion for excellence, a passion for sanctity, to be a provider, nurturer, etc. But there are disordered passions, which, if acted upon, will take us away from the beauty of our humanity and the possibility of being like our Lord.

Let's say you see a beautiful woman and are attracted to her. This is not a sin in and of itself, but if your desire modifies and you begin to want her, make efforts to entice her, or feel she must be yours, regardless of the fact that you are married or that she is married, then it becomes sin. This is a disordered passion, and if you act upon it, you will not only impact your own spiritual life, you will likely destroy numerous lives in the process. Infidelity rarely impacts the consenting adults alone. Disordered passions connected to the deadly sins must be countered with temperance. We have to learn how to say no as children, and we have to continue to practice saying no to passions that are disordered as adults.

God's Spirit within each of us at baptism is no ethereal wisp having little impact upon our daily lives; rather, the very Spirit with Jesus in ministry and culminating in his salvific work is with us in our periods of temptations and trials. When we face trials that seem overwhelming, we need to remember to beg for the grace to will the good in the moment.

We receive graces through prayer and the sacraments. Prayer is general in its application of graces. For example, you can pray at any moment for self-control in a particular area, and God extends true graces to you in that moment. The graces enable you to act in a manner worthy of the name by which you were called.

The sacramental graces given are specific, according to their particular qualities. I don't go to the sacrament of reconciliation because my Pittsburgh Steelers didn't make the playoffs, unless my behavior is so unruly that I trashed someone's property in response. Specific graces are given in the sacraments so we can grow into the saints we are called to become. Sin, and in this case a lack of self-control, is countered by willing the good in a particular case. With graces in our lives, which are not necessarily felt, we can will a good.

What is the good? That which enables us to be the saints we are called to be. How do we know the good? We form our consciences by listening to our elders, our Church and her teachings, the saints and their lives, the Scriptures, and even wise council from family and friends. Willing the good is doing the right thing in a particular situation, not in and of ourselves, but with the graces we've received through prayer and sacraments.

There may be feelings running contrary to the good, but grace gives us the power to do the right thing. Therefore, if my vice is alcohol, I need to pray and obtain graces through the sacraments, willing the good (sobriety) even if I feel a desire for that which is the opposite of self-control. I know the good because of my past, the meetings attended, and the witness of others before me. Willing the good is the hardest thing for anyone to do with self-control issues, but it is possible because of grace. We must beg for grace and will the good *in the moment.*

We will never be done implementing self-control in our marriages until we are in the grave. We always have a chance to grow in self-control because we so often want to be self-gratified, self-preserving, and self-serving. We can only combat this through the grace of God. The more we allow Christ into our lives, the more we will be self-sacrificing, self-donating—and selfless.

Activity

Ask yourself: "Are there things in my life that are out of balance or extreme behavior? How can I see Christ bringing me into a proper balance? Can I think of something I could do for my spouse that has nothing to do with me? In other words, can I do something that will spoil them?"

If something comes to mind, let that be your activity.

Chapter Six

Communication

This sixth basic quality of a solid marriage involves communication. While the other areas have a connection to a cardinal or theological virtue, this attribute is likened to the importance of prayer in our relationship with God. Without communication, a relationship suffers and withers.

Linda

"Communication is key." We often hear this said when discussing marriage. However, the truer statement would be: "*Proper* communication is key." Couples communicate every day, but we should be concerned with *how* and *what* we are communicating. Do we tell our spouses we love them no matter what, or do we express our disappointment and irritation with them? Do we communicate interest or apathy for their well-being? Are we simply residing in the same house, informing each other of day-to-day responsibilities, or do we genuinely communicate our full selves, both the good and the bad qualities, with the love of our life? Having the skills to properly communicate with our spouses does not come naturally and may take a lifetime to truly perfect, but it is necessary if your marriage is to have the longevity and joy you desire.

There are two points to consider when learning to properly communicate with your spouse. First, you must learn to communicate love and understanding in a language your spouse can understand. Chris and I are very different, and he feels love in different ways than I do. Chris is a talker; I am not. Chris uses words to share his love; words don't leave a big impression on me. If we didn't understand this fact about each other, we would be miscommunicating our love constantly. I learned early on in our marriage to *tell* Chris I love him. I need to verbally tell him that he makes me happy. I need to tell him that I am sorry. I have had to work hard at being aware of how Chris sees a situation and communicate my feelings to him in a way he can understand. The same goes for him. Quality time is more important to me. I don't just need to hear that he loves me; I need proof. It is because Chris has learned this fact about me that he created the "Spoil Linda Rotten Day." He knows I need time alone with him, having the attention on me, doing what I want to do. It doesn't require a lot of money, nor does it need to use up an entire day. It's really just the recognition that I am important enough to spoil with his full attention and effort.

There are a lot of good sources out there that can teach a couple about "love languages." I firmly believe this should be a part of any marriage prep class. We must learn how each other feels love and then work to communicate that clearly.

The second point to consider when learning to properly communicate to your spouse is the fact that you must communicate *fully* with each other. *There should be no secrets*. I am shocked when I learn about the secrets couples keep from each other. And I am not just referring to the big ones. Women lie to their husbands about how much money they spent on a piece of furniture. Men are dishonest about work or finances in order to "save face" with their wives. Both spouses too often lie to each other for "the benefit of the children." All lies are little cracks that ultimately add up and cause a break in the foundation of a marriage.

I am aware that the truth can often be painful. By keeping something from your spouse, you think you may be protecting your spouse from a painful reality. Or you may just be too weak to admit your own failings. However, I am a believer in sharing *everything*. Truth and honesty is always the better path. Pain may be a result of communicating the truth, but healing is impossible without it.

Chris and I have always practiced raw honesty in our marriage. We keep no secrets from each other. Years ago when I was teaching elementary school, I found myself slipping into the temptation of caring too much about what my principal thought about my looks. *I wonder if he will think I'm cute in this dress?* would cross my mind as I was getting ready in the morning. Now, there was no infidelity in my thoughts. I didn't linger on them, but it bothered me that I was having them at all. This little dark flaw in my character embarrassed me, and I knew Chris would probably be hurt if I told him. However, I also knew that little dark secrets, no matter how small, can grow into large dark nightmares. Secrets have power, and I did not want anything having power and control in my marriage.

So I humbly admitted to Chris that I was having these crazy thoughts—and to my surprise he understood. He told me that he loved me and that my thoughts were pretty normal. Wow, the weight was lifted immediately, and those thoughts never returned. Looking back, I can see how the enemy's temptation was not physical infidelity, but secrecy. If he could get me to hold back just one little secret from my husband, he could grow that into far worse transgressions against my marriage.

The proper timing of communication is also important. When Chris and I were first married, we read a few books dealing with marriage and family. Over and over, we read the example of the husband coming home from work and the couple sitting on the couch together, looking into each other's eyes, ignoring the children, and taking several minutes to share about their day. The point was that communication between the spouses should take priority over other things, including children. Though I fully agree with the motivation behind this teaching, Chris and I have never been able to accomplish this. In fact, the few times we tried it, we just sat looking at each other and laughing. It didn't feel natural to us. Gradually, as we learned more about each other and the ways we function, we learned more effective ways to find the proper time to share with each other about our days.

The first method we embraced was date nights. Dating couples know how to go out and spend time together sharing and talking. However, it seems that often, once married, the dating stops. Yet Chris and I have found that not only do we still enjoy going out on dates, we *need* those dates. Our busy lives and the distractions that bombard us require that we set aside special moments to reconnect. When the children were young, we still were able to find babysitters, usually Grandma or one of the aunts. Even having to pay for a babysitter was a worthwhile investment. And eventually our children grew old enough to either stay home alone or babysit the younger ones, which gave our marriage a whole new sense of freedom. Hang in there if you are not quite there!

During our dates, Chris and I make a clear effort to talk. We don't just share the events of our day or the needs and concerns of the children. We also talk about the things that weigh on our hearts, both the good and the bad. I've been asked many times, "So, Linda, tell me something you have never told anyone before." Yet after all these years, I cannot think of anything that I have not already told Chris. We have learned so much about each other during these date nights!

The other effective way we have established proper timing in communication is what I call the "Give a warning" approach. I know Chris well enough to know that when he walks in the door from work or a trip, the first thing he wants to do is check his mail. I suppose that comes from years of being paid by receiving checks in the mail. He is always hoping to find money there. Next I know Chris is going to want to unpack and wander around the house, picking up any stray garbage he can find. I guess he has a need to bring order to his feelings of disorder. The faster he gets his stuff and random things in order, the faster he can actually relax. Knowing Chris's quirks allows me to give him the time and space he needs.

Once he gets to that point, I have my chance to give him his warning. I know he may still not be able to relax enough to listen to his wife with the attention that I really want him to have, so I let him know that when he has a moment, I would like to chat with him. If it's not serious, I let him know this so he doesn't panic with worry. That warning from me gives Chris the chance to finish the things he needs so he can give me the attention I need. He does the same for me. He knows that the middle of a homeschool lesson or when there is a sink full of dirty dishes are not good times to discuss his frustrations or concerns. With a warning from him, I can wrap up what I am doing in order to give him my full attention.

In the end, proper communication in marriage requires well-communicated love and raw honesty. The lines of communication must be left wide open, not hindered by white lies or misunderstood love or poor timing. Seek to find out how to love your spouse more, and be honest about who you are—even your struggles.

Chris

If you've heard it once, you've heard it a thousand times: Communication is key for any relationship to be a success. There is no getting around the necessity of being able to talk with one another about worries and frustrations, hopes and dreams. Many times we get used to sharing our worries with co-workers or friends who regularly respond to what we are saying in a way we appreciate. For many in the workplace, the idea of repeating everything later to your spouse that you've already processed throughout the day with your peers seems unnecessary or exhausting. But we must remember our early beginnings as a couple.

Before the age of cellphones and the Internet, we (old people now) used to use this device that was put up to the ear and attached with a long coiled cord to the wall. This device was called a telephone, and, no, you couldn't look at apps or press a flat screen; instead you had to put your finger into a hole and manually dial the numbers you needed to either remember or look up in a gigantic book. Those wanting privacy would stretch the long cord as much as possible, all the way to the garage or the neighbor's house if at all possible. The conversations would be lengthy, usually until our parents yelled at us to go to bed, come to dinner, or get in the car. What did we all talk about? Pretty much anything and everything. I think there was something beautiful about just hearing each other breathe. (Yes, I realize people go to jail for calling someone and breathing in the telephone.) Linda and I would pass notes to each other in between classes, and I would even record my love for her into a tape recorder in the evenings when we were no longer allowed to talk to each other on the phone. We were in love, and we couldn't *not* talk to each other. We had to communicate our every thought and dream, and in reality it was effortless.

What I've noticed over the years is that I still love to talk with Linda. It isn't always effortless, though, especially with nine children, a three-year-old destroying the house at any given moment, teens deciding they need their mother to help write research papers for them, sports photographs that need to be ordered, plays and concerts to attend, laundry and dishes to clean, grass to mow, rooms to clean, life to live. What probably happens to you, as it does to us, is that we wake up early and move from one crazy scenario to the other until we collapse in bed at midnight. You might think we just need to have better priorities, but I suggest you walk for a minute in our family's shoes and see if you still think the solution is only in juggling a few things.

Our communication is sometimes a reminder to pick up groceries, to hurry and get in the car because we're late for Mass, or simply, "I'm going to the basement to watch football." If we are not careful, our communication can become brief internal dialogue, or a pent-up critique that just finally makes an untimely appearance. What happens to most families in the thick of battle (I mean *life*), is that we become too busy to communicate. I guarantee that if we fall into that trap, our busyness will be a catalyst of division.

Linda and I are in the habit of going to the trail near our home together. It is a place of oasis and calm for both of us amidst a constant barrage of noise. She usually walks and I run, and this act that we do together but also separately is a communication of sorts. We allow one another to get our heads on straight, and then usually we talk a little about what God has shared with us during our alone time. You could look at our conversation topics throughout the year and find a steady consistent theme, or it could seem scattered and crazy. For us, talking to each other doesn't have to be spiritual at all times or even serious; rather, it just has to be us talking. This year Linda has communicated her desire for a huge mill band saw. There is no way I can get that for her yet, since the one she wants will likely take up the entire backyard, but soon we hope to find one we can purchase. We want to make our own lumber, build our own benches, barns, stables, and maybe even a log cabin. Why? Because it is what we have been talking about for the last couple of years. We have talked about owning a farm, about homesteading and hay, bees and cattle, clearing land and healthy living. We have talked about mysteries and the BBC, good coffee and the beauty of England. Talking helps us to redefine what we think, what we want, and even where we want to be as a couple. It is essential for the health of our marriage

Unfortunately, there are false perspectives people can have about communication, and these can affect both people who have been married a long time and those who are newlyweds.

False Perspective

One of the common false perspectives about marriage is that our spouse knows already that we love them so we don't need to articulate it. They already know what we want, what we are interested in, so why bring it up? This is a recipe for disaster, because we are always growing and rethinking the way we do things and the beliefs that we hold. We are not the same people we were a year ago, and that change didn't happen at a particular moment in time. Changes are occurring in each of us all the time, and the more a couple talks, the better chance those changes have of being positive experiences. Why? Because they will be worked through together.

Another false perspective is that we all speak in the same way. Part of our job as couples isn't just giving information, as if a simple glance at the instruction manual gives you a clear understanding of the reasons an airplane of such weight can soar through the air with such grace. We couples are complex beings, and we will likely communicate to one another in a variety of ways. Learning this about your spouse will take a lifetime. There is often an assumption that your spouse means the same thing as you do when he or she speaks about a topic, when in reality you both mean two different things. You need to be perceptive and dig deeper. While your wife may say she is fine with staying home instead of going out to dinner, what she really might be saying is, "Please take me out since I've spent the last few days trapped with small children demanding I cater to their every cry!"

Another false perspective about communication in a marriage is that there is just nothing worth *saying*. People think that after a hard day of work they deserve time to themselves, so there is no need to pursue a dialogue with one another. We might feel that our spouse just nags all of the time anyway, so why try to talk about something we'd like to do? Did you need a special reason to speak to your spouse when you first met, when you were dating and falling in love? No—and you don't have to have a pressing reason to communicate with your spouse now. What you need is a new way of thinking.

A New Way of Thinking

Have you ever wondered, What language are you speaking? Sometimes it does seem that men are from Mars. We all communicate differently with one another, and I would highly recommend exploring more about this in the book *The 5 Love Languages* by Dr. Gary Chapman.

Most people assume I am an extrovert because of my public ministry, but the reality is that I am a functioning introvert. I become exhausted working and talking, and there is nothing more centering than just being alone and quiet. That being said, I need to process things with Linda, which for me is talking through an issue. It is very healing for me to put into words what is bothering me and have Linda give me council. Usually I like to sit by myself, and often that helps put things in perspective. I woke up this morning and took my sons to school and have been in the basement with no sounds for the last couple hours, and it has been a peaceful period of refueling for me. My wife is very similar. She refuels while she sits in the kitchen nook, when she walks quietly on the trail, or when she rides her bike along the path by the river. We know this about each other; it is a language we both speak. There are times we are not speaking the same language. When that happens, the key is for both spouses to verbalize their needs, wants, fears, concerns…in other words, continue developing a relationship.

I have connected the previous qualities of a good marriage with a cardinal or theological virtue. I connect this quality of communication simply to prayer, which is basically just talking to God and letting him talk to you. If you are not communicating with God, it means you are not praying, and if you are not praying, you will not grow in your walk with the Lord. As is the case in a couple, with God you can't assume that you have nothing to say—because we know that God cares about every detail of our lives! Prayer is not just about us talking to him either; rather, it is about being receptive to the words Jesus speaks to *us*. The communication is varied—experienced in the words of Scripture, the teachings of the Church, the beauty of creation, or even the groans of a prayer from the heart. God knows we need him, and he is always inviting us to enter into dialogue with him. The relationship with our spouse is meant to model this constant dialogue because love wants to know everything about the other, so that love can minister and be present to that other. We in our marriages have the chance to love each other with our presence and with our words.

A quick biblical example of this communication is Mary bringing the needs of those at the wedding feast in Cana to Jesus. We must be like Mary and bring the needs of our family to Jesus. In order to do this, we need to talk to our spouses and our children so we know where they are. You won't accidentally find out the deep parts of your spouse's heart, so ask, seek, and knock at their hearts, just as the Lord asks and seeks, and knocks at yours. This type of communication is what we need in our relationship with God, and it is what we need with our spouses.

Activity

Ask yourself: "Am I holding back something from my spouse? What can I communicate to my spouse that will take away the power of a potential sin? What can I do to communicate more? How can I get the lines of communication open?"

Talk about your first date, your first house, your first meal or movie together. Then talk about the first gifts you bought for each other, the experience of your first child, or the first time you moved. Think back to what it was like for you as a child—your favorite soda, your favorite television show, or your favorite park—and tell your spouse all about it. Encourage one another to remember and then to share. You'll have a blast.

Chapter Seven

Pursuing Dreams Together

The seventh basic quality of a solid marriage deals with the importance of pursuing dreams together. This attribute connects to the theological virtue of hope. The importance and beauty of hope in our relationship with God should be reflected in our relationship with our spouses. We hope because we believe we are loved.

Linda

We are never too old to dream. Do you have wants and desires hidden deep within your heart? Have you shared those with your spouse? Any marriage, whether it is new or old, healthy or troubled, can benefit from dreaming together. Taking time to discuss those hidden desires and dreaming about your future not only helps you both to learn more about each other, but also cements you together in a common goal. Chris and I have been dreaming together for years, and it has done more to spark new life in our relationship than anything else. This involves both the actual dreaming and then the doing.

Several years ago Chris and I started a journal we called our dream book. We sat down at our favorite coffee shop and started writing. At first, it felt awkward. I didn't think I had any dreams. I was pretty satisfied with my life. But then, I took away the barriers in my mind and let the ideas flow. I wanted to travel and eat amazing food, so I wrote, "I want to eat my way through Europe." I wanted to get healthy, and I always liked to bike when I was a kid, so I wrote, "I want a bike." I worried about my kids' relationships with God, so I wrote, "I want my family to be saints." Of course, I knew that all of these dreams could not be attained quickly, but that's why they are dreams. I see them as little points of focus that could help lead my life into the direction I ultimately want.

Our first dream-book entry that we made happen was a trip to Rome. When Chris learned of my dream to "eat my way through Europe," he got on the computer and checked into flight options. And he discovered that he had enough frequent flyer miles to get us two tickets to Rome. It was the trip of a lifetime! We spent fifteen days without kids or work in the most amazing city on earth. Without those distractions and responsibilities, we had a chance to learn more about each other.

After all those years, we finally figured out how to combine our two very opposite approaches to an adventure or trip. I have always needed to have a game plan and map out a route when we've undertaken a nice trip, such as taking the family to Disney. But Chris likes to wing it. He prefers to just see how the day unfolds without stressing about following a plan. In Rome, we finally learned how to work those two approaches together. We would start out our day with my key points of interest in our plan and then just flow with the rest of the day. I didn't care what we did as long as we made it to the couple of things I had planned for that day.

There was one day on which both of our approaches paid off beautifully. We had managed to find all of the tourist spots I wanted that day, and then in the evening, as we wandered around the city center, we decided to stop at the Church of the Gesù, where Mass was just starting. It was such a great experience to join in Mass, despite the fact that we couldn't understand what was being said. The Mass is the Mass, no matter where you are.

Afterward, Chris and I checked out the stunning church. I was admiring the most beautiful crucifix I had ever seen when I heard someone say behind me, "Mrs. Padgett?" I turned around and saw a girl who knew us from the university where Chris taught. It was surreal. There we were in the middle of another country, and we saw someone we knew from home. It turned out to be a huge blessing for us. She introduced us to several amazing priests in training and led us to many other places. If I had insisted on keeping my day tightly planned out, I would have missed out on the best surprise of our trip.

On the other hand, my planning did serve an important purpose. Chris realized this to be true the evening we met an American couple who was in Rome on their honeymoon. They were so relieved to find someone who spoke English because they had been wandering all day, lost. They had left their hotel that morning without noting its name or the street it was on. This couple had no way to find their way back, and they were clearly exhausted. We led them to the bus station in hopes that someone there could help guide them. I was stunned at their lack of common sense and planning. And Chris was instantly grateful for mine.

When we fit our two opposing approaches together, Chris and I got what we needed and enjoyed ourselves to the fullest. Why did it take us so long to figure that out?

We look for ways to share our dreams. A couple of months after our Rome trip, Chris and I visited Michigan, and he bought a bicycle from a friend. I was so mad! I said to him, "Hey, getting a bike was *my* dream, not yours." But in his mind, he just wanted to join me in my dream. My little temper tantrum got me a brand-new bike for Mother's Day, and we have loved riding together every since. My favorite date is biking about twenty miles down the trail along the Ohio River with my husband. We may look odd to those seeing us in our spandex, and our bottoms may hurt a ton, but the chats combined with soaking in the beauty of creation makes me completely happy.

Identifying our dreams can bring wonderful surprises. The most amazing thing for me is that I wanted to get a bike because I knew it would be a good exercise option for me, but what I discovered was that it awoke in me a deep love of an activity I had enjoyed doing as a young girl. I had rediscovered a part of myself that had been hidden for years. That one dream-book accomplishment has led our family into a whole new direction I could not have accomplished if I had planned it. Bike riding, visiting trails, running, and skiing are activities that our family regularly participates in—all because I wrote down "bike" in our dream book.

Dreaming together provides a great platform for a couple to really get to know each other. Even after years and years of being married, I am still learning about my husband, and he is still learning about me. Dreaming causes us to dig deeply into our inner longings and find the parts of us that have been buried along the way. Life and time have a way of covering up portions of our hearts that seem to be insignificant. More pressing matters and regular life emergencies take priority, and eventually we become used to living without those little pieces of our dreams. Having those portions rediscovered adds a spark of excitement to life. Even though I am thrilled to learn about Chris, I also have been excited to learn about who I am. You see, there is really no possible way for my husband to fully understand me if I don't understand myself. And of course, that goes both ways. It's exciting to see Chris discover the way he works and processes better. It gives me a better appreciation for the depth of his character. It gives me more to love.

Another aspect of dreaming together that adds life to a marriage is the fact that dreaming can bring unification. If you feel like your marriage is drifting apart, find a common dream to work toward together. Find something you both have as a goal. Is it better health? Is there a trip that you want to make that requires an active effort of savings in order to bring it to pass? Do you want to see your family grow closer together? Then plan activities that will promote union and love. Keep in mind that the dreams you dream do not need to be huge. Making a garden in your backyard or redecorating a master bedroom can be fun projects that lead to unity. The dream to discover local natural beauty or wanting to learn to play a new card game as a family are simple enough activities worthy to be placed into your dream book. There are no rules. If it's a dream, then it gets written down.

Even if a dream is really is just for one of you, that dream can still be unifying. What if your husband wants to try a new direction with his job or your wife wants to write a book? The encouragement that they receive from you not only builds them up in love, it also unites you two together. Being the cheerleader can often be just as inspirational as being the one attaining the dream. There is no place for attitudes or comments that set you apart from your spouse's dream, such as, "Well, if you weren't writing your book, we could go to this..." or "I don't see why it's so important for you to take this extra training just because you want to learn a new skill." Thankfully, Chris knew from the beginning of our dreaming that his participation in my dreams was just as important as dreaming his own dreams. He joined me in my biking, and I help edit his books. We work together for each other's benefit, without holding grudges or making critical remarks.

In the end, dreaming is so important on the journey to learn about who you both are. Dreaming helps uncover those hidden parts of our hearts. And fully understanding ourselves helps us be better spouses. When we know our own hearts and desires, we can better communicate them to our families, giving them the opportunity to know us better and help us accomplish those dreams. However, a dream book full of ideas can only take your relationship so far. The actual fulfilling of those dreams is where the miracles can happen. A bonding and encouragement that sometimes is difficult to manufacture in our busy daily lives can occur through the active accomplishment of a dream. This is a part of marriage that can bring the most joy. There is so much work involved in making good marriages, yet a dream book is an adventure. You never know where your dreams will lead you and your family.

Chris

Do you remember dreaming about what your marriage would be like? Maybe things started off in a wonderful way, with a perfect wedding and amazing honeymoon, or possibly you decided to get married for reasons that were less than ideal. I want to share with you another quality of a successful marriage that will help you right where you are: dreaming together. I connect this quality with the theological virtue of hope.

Linda and I often spend time dreaming together, about everything from what type of house we would live in to the amount of kids we might have, from jobs I would take to the trips we would like to go on. Have you ever thought about what you would do with lottery winnings? Or what would happen if all of the sudden you became a huge star overnight? We all dream about amazing things on our own, especially when we are kids. I would pretend to make the game-winning shot while playing basketball at the neighbor's house. I pretended to be one of the Apple Dumpling Gang—or imagined that, once the Underoos were on, I was Aquaman or Batman. Dreaming on your own is very special and unique to your own preferences, but there is something amazing about dreaming together with your spouse.

One day a long time ago, I was given a number of Lighthouse Catholic Media CDs for free because they were going to publish a talk of mine. I had a lengthy trip ahead of me, and I started going through some of the talks along the way. I decided to listen to a Matthew Kelly talk on the "Seven Levels of Intimacy," figuring that, since I'd never heard him before, I could see what all the fuss was about. I quickly decided that the first chance I got I would play this CD for my wife. I felt like I'd possibly heard the most important marriage talk of my life, even though it wasn't intended to be a specific marriage talk. I also decided that there was one thing I especially had to do because of Matthew's presentation, and that was to begin a dream book with my wife as he suggested.

If there has been one thing that Linda and I have implemented in our life that has had a profound and powerful impact on our marriage, it is this idea of intentionally writing down and pursuing the fulfillment of one another's dreams, both individually and collectively. In fact, helping your spouse fulfill their personal dreams usually results in them becoming yours as well. I won't go into this too much because Linda has already shared about her love for bikes and our dream trip to Europe, but we have dreams about other books to publish, speaking events that would be amazing, and even quitting certain vices and implementing other virtues.

My wife decided to take this obsession to another level a few years ago. She calls the family's dreams our bucket lists for the year. Every child who is able to communicate their dreams writes down the ten to twenty things they want to accomplish throughout the year. Then we as a family try to help them fulfill each one. We have run races together, taken long bike rides, attended football games, and read books so that one of us could check off another dream. What amazing memories for our family!

Much of what keeps us from dreaming together as a couple and as a family comes from holding on to false perspectives about what family life will inevitably be like.

False Perspective

So often people seem to cling to what they are used to, and it can be difficult for people to try something new. When Linda decided she wanted to get a bike and pursue her childhood love of riding, I could have thought, *Her dreams are her dreams, and mine are mine. She can do the girl things like riding a bike or walking on a trail, and I'll do guy things like going hunting and joining a fantasy football league.* That type of thinking stems from a false perspective. I decided that I wanted to be with Linda in her dream of riding bikes, so I got one to join her on the pursuit of all the rails to trails we could find. Every opportunity we had, we would ride bikes. I found that I actually liked riding, too, and if it hadn't been for Linda's dream of going back to her childhood roots, I would never have considered seriously getting on a bike again, especially wearing spandex!

Another false perspective is that we no longer have time or money to dream. Or maybe we can dream, but it is too hard when we realize that none of our dreams can come to fruition, so why try? This is a false perspective. You need short-term dreams and big life dreams. There is no right or wrong list, just naming the dream so that you can pursue it together. You may want to say, "I want to play baseball." But instead you think, *I'll never be a professional baseball player, so I may as well give up my dream of playing in the majors.* Well, if you are in your late thirties, it is probable you won't make it to the big leagues, but so what? Do you love the game or not? Do you have a blast sitting for hours spitting sunflower seeds in the dust or not? Do you like to spit? Then join an adult league and have a blast! We have to have a new way of thinking if we are going to grow as couples.

A New Way of Thinking

I remember having the chance to join the church baseball team while I was living in Florida. I had a lot of nervous energy about the whole thing because I liked the community of people, but I wasn't so sure I wanted the commitment. I enjoyed playing baseball, but I never felt like I was in the zone, especially since my childhood experiences only included occasional whiffle ball games and a softball league I was made to join—and no, I don't know if I was the only guy on the team! I joined the church team that season and had a blast. Linda was there the whole time, and in a weird sort of way, her cheering me on in the stands was a feeling I'd never really had before. I never played sports, except golf and there were no cheerleaders for that, and to have my wife cheer me on while I got up to bat was a pretty cool feeling. I could have said no to that silly opportunity to dream, but we both said yes, and it was really fulfilling.

Dreams don't have to be huge to become fond memories. Linda wanted chickens, so we bought some chicks at the tractor supply store, and they give us eggs to enjoy daily. I decided to build the little girls a chicken coop, and Linda's logical mind made sure the thing actually stood solidly upright. We dreamed about what it would be like to have a mini farm in our backyard, and that's what you'll find when you come to the Padgett home. We dreamed this together, and we continue to dream together because it brings us joy.

In a wonderful way, this is such a picture of what it means to have hope as a Christian. Hope isn't about always getting what you want; it's about dreaming together with God about the life he puts before you. We believe God is there, and we hope for joyful sanctity, and regardless if all of our dreams are checked off at the end of the year, we know that he loves us. Faith, hope, and charity are a part of what it means to be in a relationship with God, and as we have seen so far, they are certainly part of what it means to be in a relationship with your spouse. Do you dream together? Do you have hope for small and little things? This is so important, because if you are dreaming and assisting your spouse in fulfilling their own dreams, you will find each day brings new possibilities.

Activity

Ask yourself: "What are my dreams? What are my spouse's dreams? How can we help each other to achieve these dreams for the joy and enrichment of our entire family? Does all of this bring me hope for our future together?"

As I learned from Matthew Kelly, get yourself a dream book, and put your dreams in it. It's that simple!

Chapter Eight

Believing in One Another

The eighth basic quality of a solid marriage involves believing in one another. We may take this as a given or take it for granted, but it is an attribute that is connected with the theological virtue of faith. To believe in one another helps spouses to find acceptance, regardless of our imperfections. We are empowered when our spouse believes in us.

Linda

When Chris and I were in college in West Palm Beach in the late 80s to early 90s, most of the downtown was filled with rundown, drug-filled, slum houses. The surrounding neighborhood was very dangerous at night, when police sirens filled the night air and every corner was occupied by either a prostitute or a crack dealer. Chris and our good friend John would walk these streets nightly sharing the Gospel with any junkie, prostitute, or other individual they would meet. We were all aware of the dangers of walking those streets, but it was an exciting time, as we came into our own with our relationship with Christ. Radically serving God was all that mattered.

Chris and I had been dating almost three years at this point, and we often talked about getting married and dreamed about what our life would be like. One day, we were driving through the streets of this local neighborhood, and Chris pointed out a house that was similar to all the others on the street. The house was one of those condemned, weathered ones that most likely housed all of the nightwalkers. In all sincerity, he said, "I may not be able to give you a house like this one day, but we will have a life of adventure, living it together for Christ." To us poor college students, even an old ugly house like that seemed out of our reach. We look back on that statement and laugh. I understood his point. Being together, living this crazy life, and serving God in the most radical way he desires for us was our future. And so it has been. What a ride! It has been better than I ever could have dreamed. Chris has even given me a much better home in which to raise our children, and the adventure of serving God together has never been boring.

In those early days of idealism and youthful energy, I believed in Chris and he believed in me. We knew that God's calling in our life would lead us down paths we had not conceived. However, the real miracle of these times is that, despite the years that have been added and the wear and tear of life and its trials, we still believe in each other. Sure, we know each other's weaknesses and shortcomings. Sure, we have times of frustration and irritation with each other that can lead us to be mean and unloving. But when all of those moments settle down, in the end, we have each other's back. We are each other's best friends, and best friends believe in each other.

There are many compliments I can give to my husband. He is talented, handsome, loving, and a great father. But the one part of him that I think leaves the greatest mark on my life is that he inspires me. He makes me want to be a better woman. He makes me want to seek God more. He inspires my creativity, spirituality, and virtue. This inspiration does not come to me because I find him perfect. He has not set himself up on a pedestal, claiming to be the prime example of all things good. No, he inspires me instead through humility and service. He inspires me through love and gentleness. But mostly, he inspires me because he believes in me.

I have no cheerleader like Chris. Too often, actually, I feel like he overdoes his compliments, looking at me through rose-colored glasses. Yet, even though I know that his high opinion of me is not always merited because I can be selfish, mean, and proud, I have reaped the benefits of his encouragement. There is no doubt that I am the woman I am today because I have been spoiled with the love and encouragement of my husband. His belief in me gives me super powers to go beyond my comfort zone.

Last year, I felt called to begin blogging. I have so many opinions and thoughts I want to share with others, and I figured starting a blog would give me an outlet to do that. I prayed about it for a solid month before I even mentioned it to Chris. Why? Because I knew that he would automatically say, "Yes, do it!" I knew perfectly well that Chris would encourage any endeavor I wanted to try, but I first needed to know that I really wanted to do it and that God was leading me in that direction. In truth, I naturally come with an oversized ambition in life, but it's Chris's belief and love of me that gives wings to all that I set out to accomplish.

Many may think that Chris and I are just the lucky ones, that being two individuals who mutually encourage each other is a rarity and a roll of the dice. Really, I don't think so. If you want your wife to have more faith in you and the endeavors you seek to accomplish—or you feel like your husband is too critical of your work—try changing your focus. A woman's belief in her husband, especially when it's communicated in a love language he can interpret, can cause a chain reaction that can transform him more into the man you desire to see him become. If you believe in him, he will start believing in himself, and things will start happening. The same goes for your wife. If you want her to be more of what you want her to be, try loving her and encouraging her as she is. The feeling of success breeds motivation, motivation causes action, and action brings change.

Criticism of your spouse is not the best way to bring about transformation. Rather, being the best version of yourself and encouraging the other in their attempts at everything they do not only inspires improvement, but can bring about a renewal in your marriage as a whole.

Chris

I can receive the applause of thousands and still find myself empty. I can also hear a million reasons why something can't be done but somehow be motivated to pursue the task at hand. In both cases it is all about my wife and her belief in my gifts and talents. It may seem small-minded, but for me, this is the truth: I am unstoppable when Linda is behind me, and I am unsettled and unsure when she is not. The whole world's opinion will not matter to me if my wife does not believe in me. She knows me best and sees all my flaws, yet if she can still find a way to believe in my success, my abilities, or my potential impact, I can weather any storm. This is more than just a pep rally. A husband and wife must truly be one another's greatest advocates. This advocacy builds trust and dependence upon one another, and you would do well to have this type of dependence with your spouse, not with some other person.

There are a number of reasons why couples struggle with this particular quality, and it is usually because of a number of false perspectives one is holding concerning the other.

False Perspective

One reason some individuals are unwilling to believe in their spouses is that those spouses have disappointed them in the past. Since they failed once, there is no way to ensure they won't fail again. Look, we tell our kids that if they don't succeed to go and try again, so how much more is this applicable in our marriages? We will all stumble and struggle, but we must endure. Faith is a gift from God to help us believe strongly in him, even if we have failed him along the way. When we apply this in marriage, believing in one another is a gift from God to trust that our spouse has the potential to exceed far beyond what they imagine.

Do you remember the paralytic in the Gospels who didn't have faith to go to Jesus, but his friends did? They took him to where Jesus was, and then carried him to the roof, dug through it, and lowered their friend before the Lord. He was healed that day because his friends believed. We need to have that type of faith for our spouse's success. We need to believe that in Christ they are capable of greatness.

Another false perspective is that, since we have approval and acceptance from friends and employees, we don't need to have our spouse cheering us on. While the support of others is certainly important, a marriage is about two people knowing the deepest potential for both success and failings in one another. When your spouse chooses to believe in your potential for success, it's empowering.

You might have the false perspective that you are simply strong enough on your own. Sure, we might be able to make it on our own for quite a distance, but I am of the opinion that God wants us to go further than we ourselves ever imagined in life and in love, and our spouse helps this to happen. What we need is a new way of thinking to remedy the ramifications of these false perspectives.

A New Way of Thinking
Sometimes we just need to remind our spouses that even if they lose their job, miss their mark in some way, or just have a bad day, we will still be their greatest advocate and support. What is the truest gift of a marriage built upon a firm foundation? Unconditional love.

To be loved and supported and believed in by one's spouse is more empowering than you can imagine, because this is what it means to be a provision of grace for the other's sanctity. Make no mistake, you are called to bring your spouse to heaven. How this happens is going to be unique for each couple, but you can be sure advocating for the other is part of the proven method. To know you are not alone when you face an obstacle builds confidence, and to know that you will not be abandoned if you make a mistake builds trust. You are to be a gift for your spouse, fighting for them and believing in their potential, even when they doubt themselves. What a wonderful opportunity married couples have to impact their spouses in such a profound way.

Activity

Ask yourself: "How can I believe the best in my spouse for an upcoming event or in the midst of struggles he or she is having with self-confidence? Is there a way I can give a word of encouragement or offer my presence? Why wouldn't I?"

Share ways in which you trust and believe in each other. Say it aloud. Repeat often.

Chapter Nine

The Result: Intimacy

Intimacy is the fruit or result of the previous eight qualities put into play. Intimacy isn't about a physical connection alone, but it involves each of these attributes we have previously discussed.

Chris

I had a wonderful insight the other day. I know that sounds a bit proud at first glance, but stay with me. After twenty-three years of marriage, I have a bit of clarity on things today compared to the earlier times. When I think of the number of arguments spent around the topic of physical intimacy—and this was very real for us since I traveled often and it seemed that every time we had a marital moment Linda became pregnant—I wish I could have had this little bit of insight.

When I look back on all of the years, I don't think about the amazing sex, although let's be real, there have been some amazing moments. But my twenty-three years of marriage aren't just filled to the brim with constant sexual reflections, but with memories of all of the moments that allowed for us to have genuine intimacy. We moved from Florida to Ohio, bought a typewriter at an auction, and became Catholic, for crying out loud! The moments Linda and I share as we speak about going to Yummy's Homemade ice cream, riding our bikes more miles than we ever imagined possible, or sharing the memory of the first deer I harvested as a married man are all part of what it means to be with someone so entirely.

When I look back on everything thus far, there are moments of sexual joy and exploration, intimacy and passion, but that itself does not define what is meant by a vibrant and intimate marriage. In fact, it is probably lower on the spectrum than I would have thought possible. It is the full range of qualities we have been reflecting upon that help to lay a marriage foundation that is truly intimate, personal, and long-lasting. We must not reduce intimacy down to simply the physical, though that is in fact what many false perspectives would have us conclude.

False Perspective

The notion that intimacy is physical is not necessarily wrong; it just isn't the entirety of truth. We become so fixated upon the physical expressions that we have somehow concluded that a real relationship is basically passion and physical intimacy. Somehow this points people toward the idea that there is not a genuine need for emotional or spiritual intimacy, as well.

The other extreme false perspective might be an almost puritanical or neo-gnostic approach, which would put forth the idea that we should only have intimacy with God. Those who believe this conclude that physical intimacy isn't necessary, or is minimally necessary. There are actually some people who think that a Platonic approach to relationships is the most genuine.

Within the Catholic Church there is a dispensation given to couples who want to have a Josephite marriage, which is basically a couple living in a marriage that embodies the marital dynamic of Mary and Joseph, but this is extremely rare and certainly not because of the notion that physical intimacy in marriage is bad. Truthfully, a marriage can be annulled if a couple does not consummate the marriage. We need a new way of thinking when it comes to intimacy because the extreme that intimacy is either *primarily* physical or *anything but* physical are not going to work.

A New Way of Thinking

Intimacy in a marriage can only be fostered by living out so many of the previous qualities/basics we have discussed. Intimacy can grow physically, spirituality, emotionally and intellectually, but you have to work at each of these in turn. Intimacy is the fruit of a relationship that is functioning and thriving, and it all brings us ultimately back to love. God invites us to be fully human, and our spouse is a gift to us to enable us to truly be the unique gift we were created to be. The love one has toward their spouse, complemented by the love from the other toward them, helps a couple to live in time a reflection of the love of the Trinity outside of time. Intimacy is life-giving, and it is a gift meant for each person in a relationship.

Activity

Ask yourself: "When I think of the many memories I have had with my spouse—physical, spiritual, emotional, intellectual—

what has brought us closer together? What memories touch our hearts, our minds, bodies, and souls?"

Set aside time to share the many ways you have changed each other's lives. This intimacy has made each of you into someone unique—and made your marriage into a union that will never be repeated in exactly the same way by anyone else. Celebrate its beauty!

Part Two

A New Strategy for Living

With this new way of thinking, we must now implement a strategy for success.

What does the Church have to say about marriage? What about the Scriptures?

How did the Holy Family function? Each family is different, but there are certain things we can learn from the Church and Scripture that can help us to prepare for success.

What the Old Testament Says

If you did a broad-stroke analysis of sacred Scripture, you could make this assessment: The Bible begins with a man and a woman brought together by God and continues throughout the Old Testament with key figures who are placed within a marital context. God's self-disclosure throughout salvation history, as provider, healer, peace and creator, is also seen as husband, specifically in the book of Hosea. While this understanding of God as husband is truly a move from the traditional perspective of knowing him through the patriarchs, or seeing him as a Father trying to convince a wayward child to be obedient as we see in the prophets, Hosea shows us that this chosen people led and instructed by patriarchs and prophets is adulterous and unfaithful. We see this in the very life of Hosea himself.

Hosea is, in fact, a prophet and true to the tradition and understanding of God, having revealed himself throughout salvation history in the key figures of Abraham, Isaac and Jacob. But he is also hearing from God directly, in order to lead a people inclined to wayward behavior, much like a small child being obstinate in his disobedience. What is unique in this prophetic story is that Hosea is told to marry a woman who is unfaithful in order to model to the children of God their marital infidelity. So while many prophets paid with their lives, having been misunderstood and hurt by their fellow people, Hosea lives a life of faithfulness to a wife who is unfaithful so that God's people can see what they are doing to their relationship with God. Hosea not only remains faithful, but the agony he feels at being betrayed is not just words, but a gift from God in order to feel the Lord's heart. The heart of God is a husband who aches for his wife to remain faithful. In the Old Testament, the only thing that could end a betrothal was divorce or death, and what we see in the story of Hosea is that not only should the children of God be put to death as a consequence for disobedience, but they should be divorced as an unfaithful wife.

What the New Testament Says
In the beginning of the New Testament, we are shown a different marital image—a couple that is betrothed to one another who are a tangible witness of faithfulness. In many ways, the New

Testament offers a counter presentation of what love should look like, juxtaposed to the story of Adam and Eve and really all of Israel during times of relational infidelity toward God. Joseph and Mary are that primordial couple revisited in a way, and we find great consolation in Joseph's willingness to protect and care for that small holy family. Mary's obedience is a great relief for the student of salvation history because we see the New Eve willingly obey the heart of God and deny the offer of self-gratification. As we examine the beginnings of the New Covenant, then, we see a marriage that is brought together by God, and thankfully theirs is a new story leading to a redemption and resurrection rather than a fall and fatality.

In the second chapter of my book *Wholly Mary*, I discuss a bit more in depth the Holy Family, especially St. Joseph and his love for Mary. Here I will simply state that Joseph's love toward Mary was so like the Father's that he in many ways embodies faithful Hosea, although Mary was certainly not unfaithful. I believe that while St. Joseph didn't understand all things about Mary and her being found with child before they had come together, he may have wanted to divorce her quietly because he was overwhelmed by the singular devotion to God in a manner that the Messiah would be born of her. Even if he is a man who struggled with doubt in knowing for certain the reasons for her being with child, his desire to quietly divorce her was admirable and truly loving, especially in a time where he could have rightly ruined his seemingly unfaithful wife.

Joseph's love for Mary was entire. Mary's love for Joseph was of such magnitude that she trusted him to hear from God concerning her faithfulness. It is after the angel tells Joseph not to be afraid to take Mary as his wife that we see this couple remain steadfast, even amidst great opposition. As Adam and Eve were thrust from the Garden of Eden, we can see the Holy Family thrust from their homeland due to the evil and diabolical plans of Herod, who bathed the streets with the blood of the holy innocents in his attempt to bring death upon the Last Adam. The first Adam failed in his willingness to protect his bride from the temptation of evil and the ramifications of sin, while this man Joseph reflects aspects of the last Adam in his willingness to protect and serve the gift he has been given in Mary.

Some older literature, specifically Apocryphal books, portray Joseph as an old man, a patriarch of sorts, who is simply willing to be a fatherly figure toward Mary who has been entrusted to his care. This is certainly not the ideal picture of Joseph, whom I believe to have been a typical man of marrying age during that time in history. He was likely in his mid-to-late teens, a man with a trade who was able to take care of his betrothed. Joseph was willing to not only provide physically for his wife, but was willing to provide a place for her to live out her vow of consecration to God in a holy union that would truly have Christ present in their midst.

The reason many of the images of St. Joseph found in older literature portray him at such an old age is likely an attempt to preserve Mary's marital virginity. This is an attempt that does more harm than good as, far as I am concerned. For Joseph's heart for Mary was of such a collaborative union that he willingly embraced a life of total consecration to God's will.

Because Jesus was within the Blessed Mother, there was no need for a physical sign that would somehow testify to love. You don't need the sign when you have the fulfillment, and Jesus's presence in the marital union of Joseph and Mary was the fitting reality of their love.

The Nativity that we celebrate each year is the reminder that love became man and dwelt among us. That love was not just there for a moment and then gone; rather, that love was held and nourished, cared for and fed by Joseph and Mary. That love was seen and adored, protected and pondered for decades. It would not have been remotely fitting to have insisted that Joseph and Mary somehow prove the presence of love within their marriage by the physical marital act, because that would have reduced what was already so visible in the face of God. Jesus's presence in the Holy Couple bespeaks a love that we in marriage here and now try to model and embody in the physical act of intimacy. The marriage of Joseph and Mary was entire, total, ideal, and true. We would do well to reflect that type of devotion to Christ in our marriages.

When Jesus begins his public ministry at the age of thirty, we do not hear any more about St. Joseph, and it is probable that he has passed away. We can assume this to be the case when at the cross Jesus gives Mary to St. John, because had Joseph been alive, Jesus's giving of Mary to him would have been untenable.

As most will remember, the beginning of Jesus's public ministry is, quite significantly, at a wedding. The marriage celebrations in the first century were not like ours today, which go on for a few hours before everyone makes their way home.

Weddings in Jesus's time would go on for extended periods of time, and for the wine to run out too early would result in great shame being placed on that family. Mary's request of her son to help with the wine supply at the wedding at Cana, subtle as it may seem, is certainly more than a desire to assist a friend who has come up short in festive provisions for guests. There is more at work in this story to be sure.

For example, in Mary, we can see the New Eve at work in Cana, as well as the Last Adam in Christ. The lack of wine in this story shows and points toward the lack of preparation of Israel for the great wedding between God and man. The lack of wine shows the inability of humanity to satisfy, as well as other inadequacies and weaknesses. Jesus begins his public ministry by lavishing the wedding party with the best wine because God is always prodigal in his provision. Jesus hears Mary's, the Woman's, request and doesn't just attempt to cover the shame of the father of the bride with a temporal solution like fig leaves sown together; rather, he gives the best of wine, that is in this case never going to run out again. The witnesses of this miracle are select, and they are encouraged by the Woman, who tells them to do whatever he tells them. The fruit of the vine here brings joy and union. It is the best. The fruit of the vine eaten in the Garden of Eden brought death and division, placing a wedge between woman and man, God and humanity. It wasn't the best, but was eaten in an unwillingness to do whatever he told them, which was to not eat from the tree of the knowledge of good and evil. This a passage of Scripture is both very Eucharistic and packed with significant marital imagery.

The New Testament ends with the wedding feast of the Lamb. And there is marital imagery in the stories of Jesus in his public ministry, as well as in the Last Supper and consummation at the cross. St. Paul speaks about the union of Jesus with his Church as bride and shows how faithful marriages give a witness of this. From the beginning of Scripture to the middle until the end, marriage is important because it shows us a part of our relationship with God that is best known through the marital relational structure.

What the Church Says

We can also find a wonderful myriad of ecclesial teachings that advance the beauty of marriage. I will simply refer you to a few recent and very important documents that would be truly encouraging for you to read: *Gaudium et Spes* from Vatican II has some outstanding words of encouragement for married couples and the family as a whole, and *Humanae Vitae*, though short, has an impact that is still felt today. When many people assumed that the Church was going to suddenly change its stance on contraception, *Humanae Vitae* reinforced her commitment to the marital act's being unitive and procreative. The third document I would refer you to is *Familiaris Consortio* by St. John Paul II.

When you start to read the documents of the Church, you begin to realize that many phrases sound the same, and that is because they often are the same. The Church will regularly quote from earlier works published by previous councils and popes because the teachings of the Church are organic in their development and remain true to previous proclamations. This is part of a great gift we have been given in the Catholic Church. When you listen to the modern media, they would have you believe that things can easily be redefined or changed, according to the tendencies of the times. The Catholic Church insists that our approach to marriage and family not be dependent upon one's culture or time because this is a gift from God and not a construct of man, culture, or a particular time. We hold to the teachings of the Church because God ensures that the message given to us, by him, is worth being adhered to.

It is painful to watch someone try to build something without instructions or travel to a place without directions. We have both instruction in our Church and clear directions on how to thrive within dark times. Marriage is not left to the fickle behavior of an age captivated with selfishness because marriage is a gift from God, pointing to eternity. Thank God for the Church.

Lessons for a Lifetime

We have spoken about the various cardinal and theological virtues and their corresponding attributes for a healthy marriage and have looked at a few examples from Scripture and the Church concerning marriage. In this next section, we want to share personal stories that offer some insights important to a committed marriage. Most couples experience plenty of obstacles along the marriage journey, and finding out that we are not alone is a great consolation.

Chapter Ten

Remember to Forget

One of the problems found in marriages is the litany of offenses one is inclined to list out for the other in the heat of battle. Statements of "You always" or "You never" are always going to get you in trouble and will never help your marriage. Some people have a merciless ability to remember every offense, but going through the countless ways your spouse has let you down is not going to bring about the response and improvement you are likely looking for. So, when conflict arises in a marriage, how do we move on?

Chris

Part of this question depends upon how long a couple has been married. In the beginning of a marriage there is still so much that you are both learning about one another. There are certainly little things that irritate you about your spouse, but they usually seem manageable. For couples who have been together for a long time, however, there are patterns that repeatedly come up, and while one may promise to change their behavior, it seems unlikely that will be the case since you've both been down this same path a thousand times before. Yes, there are personality traits and difficulties from one's past, but there is one thing you can intentionally do, even if it seems to go against everything you feel inside: You must remember to forget.

Jesus gives us the model of what to do when we are offended or hurt. We are to forgive and turn the other cheek. No, I am not suggesting people stay in an abusive situation, but I am talking about how to deal with the fights every couple has along the way. It is so easy to resort to the "You always or "You never" response because this shifts any blame from ourselves to the other. It may be that the other person really is to blame and that they do always seem to fail in a certain way, but in the end you can only be responsible for your own actions. While we as couples are called to help one another to the Beatific Vision, we aren't meant to drag each other, kicking and screaming. We have to learn to forget the offenses.

I know how hard this is, and it is possible you are asking the question: But what if he never learns? Well, what if he, in fact, never *does* learn? What if she always *does* leave the cap off the toothpaste, or he always *does* leave the blasted toilet seat up? Is it possible to still love someone who can't seem to fall in step with your wants and requests? I guess what I am asking is, will you still love them in their mess?

One day I was talking to a pastor. He was taking full-time courses at the university, married with a few children, and pastoring on the weekends. He would come home, and his wife, who was a stay-at-home mother, had no interest in cooking and expected help with all the kids. He mentioned that he would watch the kids almost all the time when he was home and that his wife was not available to assist, even though he had papers to write and sermons to prepare. Things were overwhelming for him, and I could feel the frustration and desperation in his comments. Finally I asked him the question I just posed here: "What if she never changes? Will you still make the meals and do the laundry for her? Will you still watch the children?" I then went on to tell him, "If you will serve her, even if she doesn't serve you, then you will be like Christ. You would be starting every day new—nothing from the previous day would keep you from serving and loving her today."

The goal in marriage is certainly a mutual self-sacrifice, but there are times when one spouse does not seem to get that memo. And in those cases, we need to always ask the end question: "Does that mean I won't stay committed to my spouse? Is this the proverbial last straw on the camel's back? If so, why? Why this? It certainly isn't about the toilet seat or about the toothpaste, is it?"

The only way a couple can truly live together for decade after decade is to be willing to unite in the purpose of loving one another afresh each day. Putting aside the past arguments and approaching each day like it is a new opportunity is going to give you an amazing edge. People who can give the tally of how many offenses their spouse has committed are likely people who are looking for a separation. Yet those who can overlook certain quirks are working to help their marriages succeed for a lifetime—and often have a lot less tension along the way. If love is the foundation of your marriage, then your desire to be a better gift to your spouse will motivate you to change. If you can remember to forget the petty offenses, the unintended misunderstandings, the careless words, and the missed opportunities, then you will find that many things do eventually resolve themselves.

Sometimes they do not, of course, and there are seasons in a marriage in which little things mount into big issues. I am not suggesting that we just ignore all offenses; rather that we pick our battles carefully and realize that nagging and blaming will never bring the intended goal. We change when we are loved, when we are accepted, and when we are in a place of trust. We change when someone sees us and believes we are capable of greatness. We change not from who we are, but we change into becoming more authentic when our spouse remembers to forget—or forgets to remember—at least until the foundation is laid for a needed heart-to-heart.

It is that image that is important: one heart speaking to another. When you know you are loved by your spouse and they come to offer a word of correction, you know it is from their heart to yours and not out of intolerance. Yes, talk things through, but take your time in pursuing moments where you will expound upon every detail of your spouse's character faults. You should have the rest of your life to help one another along toward holiness, so you don't have to fix all of each other's faults in a single day. After all, you'll want something to do tomorrow! Or better yet, maybe just forget about some of those things altogether and start over today.

For Reflection

• What types of conflict have you encountered in your marriage?

- How have you dealt with serious disagreements?
- In your marriage, how successful have you been in letting go of past hurts?
- What are some practical ways you can show love for your spouse this week?

Chapter Eleven

To Be Seen

God has made the human person with a desire to be truly seen by another. We want to be seen as we authentically are at our core, beyond any false masks we might wear that hide our real selves.

Chris

Something very interesting happens to us as we are growing up: We begin to notice and feel attraction toward others. I am pretty sure I was not alone as a small boy in having a bit of a crush on some of the leading ladies in television and film. Lynda Carter as Wonder Woman, Valerie Bertinelli on *One Day at a Time*, Erin Gray on *Buck Rogers in the 25th Century*, and pretty much all of Charlie's Angels. They were beautiful, and, while I didn't understand all of the reasons for my infatuations, I wondered what it would have been like to be theirs and for them to be mine. Certainly, these young crushes weren't going anywhere, but I was not alone in spending many hours imagining what it would have been like if we could be together.

By the time we get to middle school or high school, there is something distinct about the manner in which we deal with our attractions. Instead of keeping our attention focused upon a mythical person whom our chances of meeting are slim to none, our senses are awakened to those right next to us in our classrooms and on the bus to and from school. We begin to imagine what it would be like to talk to them for the first time, to be seen and wanted by that potentially significant other. When the moment occurs and we are seen by the one we have fostered feelings and dreams for, it is as if we are set aright. Young love is adventurous, mythical, imaginative, and free. Everything is new, and possibilities abound for success, though we see around us flounder and fail. Young love is where we are often seen by another and accepted as we are—that is, until we are not. Young love is where we learn what works in a relationship that has attraction within the mix, and it is also where we realistically learn survival techniques to keep us from being hurt again.

We all want people to think well of us, to find us attractive, intelligent, artistic, athletic, or whatever it is we find important that month. A lot of time is spent fixing our hair just right, buying clothes that complement our figures, which we hope will be admired by some and envied by others. These acts are usually done so that we can make a good first impression. But after we find ourselves in a relationship with another, those first impressions are not as important, because they usually get to know what we are like when our hair is a mess, our clothes are crumpled, our makeup is unapplied, and our attitudes are less than ideal. It is what we long for: someone who can accept us just the way that we are, because the way that we are cannot be glossed over. What would it be like to be freed from the pressure of trying to be like what we think our significant other expects? Wouldn't it be easier and more fulfilling to have a significant other who loves to be with us, without any pressure to be what we are not?

Through the early stages of infatuations and into the young years of trying to find out who we are and longing to share that with others, there are a lot of emotions and longings, some fulfilled and some unsatisfied. When a couple finally enters into a relationship in which they accept and see one another in their vulnerabilities, there is a marked difference on the journey. To be accepted as we are and loved at the core of our being is what we were made for, and the moments we encounter it here in time are moments that point us to the ultimate relational fulfillment in eternity. In other words, God made us because he knows the most intimate and vulnerable reality of our being and longs to be with us in that. There is no need to be anything other than who we truly are because God sees the "us-ness" that we can't even see in ourselves.

Often as we are growing up, we lose sight of who we are at our core because we think that being ourselves is not good enough. The popular kids in school have the external appearance of having what we want, having masked perfectly their insecurities and vulnerabilities. Over the years, I think many of us lose who we are, trying to fit into trends that our culture fixates upon or habits we have walked in so that we can somehow feel more secure in various settings. When a young couple finds someone with whom they can let their guard down without being hurt, the "us-ness" is given freedom to step out into the light. This is a very vulnerable time for most and can even be frightening. Acceptance by one's significant other in these moments can be freeing.

A marriage that is grounded in seeing and loving each other in such vulnerable ways is one that will grow and blossom. Marriage is meant to be the safest relationship this side of eternity, and it is meant to prepare us for the ultimate moment when we see more clearly the one who has seen us entirely. When we are truly seen by our spouse, it opens up unimagined vistas for what a relationship can be. Acceptance without qualifications, without subtle expectations, that sees and allows for blips and bumps, is the necessary quality of a lasting relationship. Being seen by God is the desire of each person, and to experience this in a partner who knows our every insecurity and oddity is a taste of God's love.

To share dreams and worries, fears and faults, is something that we can do in a variety of relationships with friends and family members, but to share the most insecure parts of our lives—and our very bodies—is something that is safest with one who sees us at our core. Marriage is meant to be a place of full disclosure, grounded on the bed of trust that this person who has been given the most keen and vivid encounter with us is encouraging us to become even more ourselves. The wonderful thing about marriage is this constant opportunity to grow into who we really are. This growing cannot happen without being seen and accepted for who we are, and a spouse capable of loving the other's mess is a spouse who will walk with their partner into a new way of living. This is what we were made for—and what we long for in a relationship.

For Reflection

- What kinds of expectations does your spouse have concerning you?
- How do you deal with those expectations?
- Are there certain ways you expect your spouse to act or things you expect your spouse to do? How do you respond when those expectations aren't met?
- How could you deepen the intimacy in your marriage, making it a safe haven for your hopes and dreams as well as those of your spouse?

Chapter Twelve

Our Baby Story

The Catholic Church teaches that the purpose of a marriage is not just the uniting of two separate lives—couples must also be open to the possibility of being procreative, since marriage reflects the life and self-giving love of the Trinity. Issues surrounding having children are something every newly married couple must face.

Linda

In college, Chris and I hung around with people who were excited about their faith and believed in living a radically for God. One way that this extreme faith showed up was in their views about children and contraception. Even though we were Protestant, we were taught that contraception was against the will of God because it stifled our faith and went against the teaching in Scripture to "Be fruitful and multiply." We were all on board with this teaching until we got engaged.

During those few months of engagement, we battled with the decision to use birth control or not. Honestly, I was afraid of getting pregnant right away. Chris and I had been chaste for the last couple years of our dating, and we wanted time together without the possibility of morning sickness and a growing belly getting in the way. So in the end, we decided to go on the pill.

Within a couple months of marriage, my conscience and neurosis got the better of me. I have also always been a person who hated taking unnecessary medication. I would even suffer through a headache before I took an aspirin. So the idea of taking a pill filled with hormone-altering drugs that listed "blood clots in the lungs" as a possible side effect really freaked me out. I told Chris that I needed to get off them for my own health and sanity. Of course, Chris was perfectly fine with the idea. After enjoying a couple of months of marital bliss, we had already started getting the baby itch. After all, we had been together for nearly four years, so why not have a baby? I was almost finished with school, and Chris had a decent job. We didn't put much more thought into it than that. So the pills got thrown out, and a couple of months later, our first daughter was conceived.

After a fairly normal pregnancy and delivery, however, I basically lost my mind. My adjustment to motherhood was not easy at all. My natural obsession for perfection and order was shaken hard by the reality of a new little human who had her own ideas of schedule and neediness. It took me months and months to settle into the comfortable reality of motherhood. Eventually, I learned to relax and enjoy the gift of life we were given.

Some may find it ironic or even unbelievable that a mother of nine children had such a rough start to motherhood. But it's the truth. If God had not intervened in our baby planning—or really lack of baby planning—I don't know if I would have ever been "ready" to have another child. And then after daughter number two was born, we felt we were finished with growing our family. At that point in our life, I was working full time, and Chris was finishing his degree. We figured that we would settle down into the whole "two car, two income, two children" existence. That would have been perfectly fine, but God had other plans.

Around this time, our faith life was exploding. Chris had started a ministry, and I desperately wanted to get back home with my babies as a full-time mom. When all of that finally happened, the babies started coming more often. What changed in my heart to allow that to happen? God's faithfulness.

I used to get up early and go for a walk every morning. Those times were my prayer times. At some point, I remember having a realization about God's provision in our life. We were living this life of faith. We saw the way he provided for our food and our financial needs. We saw how he knew us better than we knew ourselves and desired to take care of us. So the great revelation that came to me, as I stared at the beautiful blue morning sky, was, "If I say I trust God with my very life, why don't I trust him with my fertility? God knows my needs more than I do. He knows what's best for me better than anyone. How can I say I give my life to Jesus and yet hold back one of my most important aspect of my womanhood, my fertility?" So the pills got thrown out once again.

Daughter number three arrived several months later, followed quickly by our first son. They are eighteen months apart. To be honest, I have vivid memories of fighting with God over the fact that I was not ready to have another baby, but God wanting me to trust him. Often idealism runs straight into the wall of realism. In those challenging times, we need grace to get through them.

As the years went on, I started to fear that my fertility would never run out and I was going to have babies forever. There were times that a positive pregnancy test was followed by lots of screaming and objects being thrown, but Chris and God are both patient with me. I always eventually fell into the rhythm of each pregnancy and grew to cherish the idea of another Padgett in the house. I love all of my children, and I can't imagine my life without any of them. God knew I needed each one to make me the woman I needed to be.

There was one time when our family was about to make a move from Florida to Ohio, and it looked like we were going to have a good deal of money from the sale of our house. We decided that we wanted to be generous to God in a new way. We knew the miracle and blessing adoption was for many families, and we also wanted to welcome a child into our home through adoption. We wanted to use this house money and be generous with a soul who needed a family to love him or her. We started looking into adoption agencies, and I felt excited about this new direction for our family and new way to show God our generosity.

But then the Holy Spirit spoke loud and clear to me one day in the kitchen, as though his voice spoke audibly to my heart. He said, "You are not going to adopt a baby. You will have more babies of your own." I literally screamed, "No!" I wanted this opportunity to show how we can sacrifice for him and serve him radically. I was also tired of the pregnancy and nursing cycle, and I wanted to sacrifice in another way. But once again, God's voice spoke clearly and said, "Linda, for you, pregnancy is the greater sacrifice, and I want the greater sacrifice." How could I argue with that? He knew me too well.

Pregnancy and children are a sacrifice. Sure, they are the most rewarding and eternal blessing God can give to your marriage, but they are a lot of work. Stretch marks, vomiting by the side of the road, sleepless nights, weight gain, and fears that you never imagined can be just a few reasons why children come with a price. However, whether it's just one or it's an entire herd, children are ultimately the reason for womanhood. They bring a fulfillment to a woman's life that nothing else can give. Children reap blessings and pour life into our marriages, especially when we allow them to change us into the better versions of ourselves.

Many couples use Natural Family Planning. This is the Catholic Church-approved means in which a couple can space pregnancies or avoid a pregnancy when there is a serious need to do so.

In recent decades, science has learned a lot about the way a woman's body works. Unlike a man who is continually fertile, a woman's fertility typically lasts only a couple of days out of a month. Science has discovered that the woman's body gives very specific signs to warn of the approach of ovulation. Modern couples have been given the gift of this knowledge to not only have some control over the size and timing of their families, but also to have a greater possibility to conceive at all when it seems that conception is harder to attain than for others.

The reason that NFP is considered acceptable by the Church, when other forms of birth control, such as the pill, condoms, and other devices or hormonal implants, are not is because the use of NFP in a marriage requires the couple to work alongside the natural functions of the body and not against them. God is the creator and designer of life. He is the one who made the woman's body to work in a rhythm that can be easily predicted. It has just taken us a really long time to learn how this masterpiece of ingenuity works. When a couple learns to detect the signs of fertility, they become better informed partners who can work in union with God's design in the planning of their family.

There is a ton of information regarding NFP out there. Most dioceses offer classes or at least can put you in contact with a trained instructor. The techniques vary from very basic to more involved, but they all boast a 96–98 percent effectiveness rate. However, the real beauty of these methods is the fact that they require the couple to communicate their goals and reevaluate their motives monthly. Birth control is not placed in the hands of just one spouse, nor is fertility placed on hold for an indefinite amount of time without paying any attention to the will of God. Sure, it requires a serious effort and times of restraint, but so does everything else in marriage. It's about the union of two people, pulling up their sleeves, getting their hands dirty, and making a very holy and important witness of God's love shine to those around us.

Chris and I have practiced Natural Family Planning during different points in our marriage. We have never used it for very extended times, which is the way it was intended for the majority of marriages. We have never had extenuating circumstances that would have required us to postpone another baby for a long length of time, or indefinitely. NFP's high rate of effectiveness applies to the times when it is used correctly or used at all. Just because we have used NFP during one month and then chose to not use it in the next does not mean that NFP doesn't work. It means that we had better reasons to not use it than to use it.

Chris's travel schedule, which has been crazy for more than twenty years, has at times made it impossible to strictly follow the guidelines of NFP. As a couple, we have chosen to just be open to whatever God has for us, even the addition of a new child, rather than step outside of his will and take our fertility into our own hands. Though there were times in the years before we became Catholic when we gave in to the convenience of artificial contraception, once we learned about the beauty of the teachings of the Church, we have remained faithful. So for us, that has meant lots of babies!

Sure, it's been difficult at times, but we don't "blame" NFP for failing us. Rather, we believe that we have used it correctly, by using its information to choose the best solution to our needs in that moment. We have had moments when the need for physical union and love outweighed any other need. On the other hand, we have had moments when the need for physical healing, mental rest, or financial stability have outweighed the other needs. NFP has taught us to consciously be aware of all of our choices and make the best one together.

Nine children, plus five other souls we will only meet in heaven, are the jewels in our crown. Books, notoriety, financial success, or material possessions cannot compare to the reward these crazy kids will create for us. The amazing truth of children is that they are the *only* thing we can do in correlation with God. He allows us to participate in his divine ability as creator to make a new life. Chris and I have given birth to fourteen babies that would otherwise never have existed if it weren't for our generosity and love. Why would we want to limit that amazing ability, just for a little more earthly comfort?

The other amazing fact about children is that they are the only "things" in this world that will go with you into the next. Not even our very bodies, which we work tirelessly on perfecting and beautifying, will go with us to heaven. They will rot in the ground. But my children, both living and lost, will be united with me forever in the most perfect place imagined, being loved by our Creator in the most perfect love ever. There is nothing that can compare to that.

Our baby story has lots of twists and turns, through lots of frustration and joy. We have allowed God to write the story that he has desired of us, and we are better people because of it. I love my crazy life and my crazy kids. I am a blessed woman.

For Reflection

- How have you and your spouse approached having children? Have you always agreed? If not, how have you worked through any differences?
- What sacrifices have you made in order to have a family?
- Have you ever used NFP? If so, what was your experience? If not, why not?
- As new parents, what challenges did you encounter and how did you deal with them?

Chapter Thirteen

Seeing God's Grace in the Turmoil

Even the best of marriages can be shaken to the core by an unforeseen event. There is no way to prepare for these difficulties, but having a solid foundation of faith in God and trust in your spouse will help you weather any storm that comes.

Linda

I became a grandmother at the age of forty-four. Yes, I still have a toddler at home, but nonetheless, it happened.

This last October, I was awakened from a sound sleep by my bedroom light being turned on and my two oldest daughters standing at the foot of my bed. My oldest daughter, Hannah, said in a very serious voice, "Mom, Sarah has something to tell you." My first thought, being that I was half asleep, was, *Who's dead? Is she going to jail for something?* I think it took me about twenty minutes of listening to my girls cry and talk before I fully realized that I wasn't actually sleeping, and this wasn't a dream.

There are many words that no mother wants to hear coming out of their teenage daughter's mouth, and among them are: "Mom, I'm pregnant." With those three short words came a flood of emotions and fears that seemingly caused my brain to explode and my heart to melt. I thought with fear, *Oh, no. She will never find someone to really love her now.* Her entire future had changed. All the dreams and thoughts that I, as her mother, held for her disappeared in the face of those few short words.

Then I came to my senses.

It didn't take long for my perspective to change. The fear was replaced with intense love and admiration for this daughter of mine who was facing a new, different future with courage and hope. She bravely accepted her mistake of premarital sex, faced the consequences, humbled herself, put her chin up, and stepped into motherhood as gracefully as anyone ever has. Pregnancy was not in her plans, but she knew that this new life was a gift of grace being poured into her future.

It's difficult for us parents to accept the fact that our children get old enough to make huge mistakes, no matter how carefully we've tried to raise them. It's hard to allow them to face the consequences of their mistakes, especially since as parents we have done everything to protect them from so many possibilities. Yet we are blessed by the way our daughter responded in her moment of crisis. We know that some well-raised children do not heed their parents' instructions, and it is not always just one person's fault, but we must keep hoping that God will do the work he needs to do in their lives. Their story isn't finished yet, and the legacy that we as parents give to our children can bring about beauty amidst turmoil and temptation if we continue to pray.

Through our situation with our second-oldest daughter, I have learned that often God uses these difficult moments in our children's lives to shine grace and mercy into the darkened areas of their hearts. I recognized that there were many ways in which the sin that our daughter was participating in could have been brought to light, but God choose the most merciful way to do that, by giving her a new life. This baby declared to the world that she messed up, but God's grace empowered her to move on with renewed hope and faith. She knows that of all the mistakes she has made in her life, her daughter is *not* one of them. This unplanned baby is not an error that will ruin her future. She is the very grace that God will use in Sarah's life to give her focus, hope, and unbelievable love that only a mother can feel.

A pregnancy was not the worst thing that could have happened in our daughter's life. And she knows all the really tragic things that could have come into her life if she had continued down the same path or chose a different solution. Her little Audrey is the opposite of those things. She is light, beauty, spiritual healing, love, forgiveness, hope, inspiration, and victory. She is a gift from her Creator, who loved her enough to not only shine light into her darkness, but overflow her with immense generosity.

Sarah's life will never be the same. This is not a punishment. This is a blessing. This is her legacy.

Chris

I was in the Diocese of La Crosse, Wisconsin, doing a youth event. It was well after midnight, and I was finally getting ready for bed when my cell phone rang. It was my wife, and I got a little panic-stricken wondering what terrible thing must have happened for her to call so late. I answered the phone, worried that someone was in the hospital or had been in a horrible car accident, and Linda began with, "I think you should sit down." Suddenly, I somehow just knew, and I blurted out, "Sarah's pregnant." She asked me how I knew, and I could only respond that I just did. I could only mutter, "My poor little baby girl." As tears flowed down my cheeks, I just agonized over the weight of this moment in the life of my daughter, who was a child herself as far as I was concerned. She will always be my little girl, and the last thing I wanted was for her to have any difficulties.

Then, as is often the case, I started being a little selfish and began to worry about what this would mean for me. We would have to move, go off somewhere remote so that no one would know that we were not a perfect family. Would I need to stop doing ministry? For crying out loud, my wife and I have written a chastity book and now my teenage daughter is pregnant. I've lost all credibility,—I, I, I, me, me, me.

I told Linda, "She is keeping the baby, and we will raise the child as one of our own." Linda was very patient with my craziness and said, "We will let her look at adoption, too, but I am not going to have a tenth baby. This is going to be her child, and she needs to realize that." I went into some crazy mode of insisting that I never be separated from my grandchild. Period.

Finally, I allowed the grace of God to calm me down, and I remembered something Father Stan Fortuna had said to me concerning someone who shared the knowledge of her unwed pregnancy with him. He shouted with joy and told her how amazing that child was, and how this baby was a gift from God. Then he said, "Your timing is horrible, but praise God for that baby." I told Linda over the phone that how we respond to Sarah in this, her most intense crisis, will be what she remembers about us for the rest of her life. She had to know that we loved her—and that our talk about a God who forgives was not just lip service. I got home a couple of days later and walked right up to my daughter and hugged her, uttering those words of praise to God for this life, and then whispered to Sarah, "Your timing is horrible, but praise God for that baby." She and I laughed.

Most of us have sins we keep hidden, and that no one will ever know except our Lord in the sacrament of reconciliation. We go to confession and they are not only forgiven but forgotten by our God. We walk out of the confessional, and all that anyone knows is that we were lost and are found, broken and now healed. The sin Sarah committed, having premarital sex, was forgiven in confession, but every month she walked about in public, attending classes, going to church visibly, showing to all that she was a teenage mom. People talked, Sarah was ignored, and she was hurt by those who were supposed to care. The majority of our town came to her rally. It has been amazing to see the impact this little baby has had on not just our family, but around the country, as many have heard about this story from my talks and Linda's blog. The legacy of Sarah's willingness to be open to life, even though it was unexpected, is visibly present for all to see. This legacy is Audrey. And she is my granddaughter.

For Reflection

- What unforeseen events have visited your marriage?
- How did you cope with these unexpected challenges?
- If you are a grandparent, what has that experience been like for you?
- Have you had to deal with a serious situation with a son or daughter? How did you respond, and what was the outcome?

Chapter Fourteen

Leaving a Legacy of Love

How will we be remembered? How have we helped form our children in their understanding of God's love by their witnessing our marriage? How have we prepared our spouse for eternity? These questions all speak to the importance of leaving a legacy of love in our marriage and family.

Chris

At this point in our marriage, our oldest is twenty-two years old and married, living in New York. Our youngest is three, and it seems like we have every other age still present in our home. I have been thinking a little about how different it will be for our children to move off and begin their own families. I am not able to even understand the arsenal of examples they have witnessed from Linda and me over the years.

My parents were divorced about forty years ago, and I think it is likely that there are still some things that I hold onto, feelings I've fostered over the years that could easily be traced back to that moment in time. What would I have been like had my mother and father stayed together? I will, of course, never know. I am absolutely thankful that I have a great relationship with my dad, and hope I can model so many of his qualities the older I get, but there were some difficult years when I was younger.

Most kids have those moments of difficulty as they enter their teen years, but it is certain that parents being a united front is helpful when encountering the challenges middle and high school kids experience. As my kids wrestle with their uncool parents, who seem to, as far as they are concerned, say No more often than not, they have realized over the years that when mom and dad say something, it is a choice made in union. In other words, they have very little hope in swaying one from the other in decision-making.

Now let's be honest, there are certainly times when my wife comes and tells me that I made a wrong decision, or overreacted, but she will come to me and tell me instead of going against me to the kids. Often because of her intercession, I go and reduce the sentence, if you will, for the particular child. It is this working together that I think is helpful for us as parents, but also for them as kids. I believe that children need to know what clear boundaries are, and that those boundaries must be the same with both parents. Usually kids rarely grow tired of pushing the boundaries if mom and dad together can remain steadfast. I know we have not been perfect over the years, but I am confident that this unity in discipline and decision-making is a gift that they will likely model in some way as adults. It is a challenge to family unity when a couple is constantly holding to differing levels of expectations, or easily manipulated by a child's pleas. Linda and I made a choice a long time ago to work together instead of at odds with one another.

I doubt any of us will really know how we will be remembered by our children, unless they write a biography, and even then their perspective is certainly one-sided. I worry that I've not represented my parents well over the years in the various written accounts or presentations I've given. Our lives are far more complex than an account given in a fifty-minute presentation at a particular point in time. We have all had good days and bad days, and it isn't often that we get to pick which ones will be remembered. For us as parents, the hope is that there are far more good days than bad, and that our children will understand that we too were very human.

If you were to come to my house, you would likely make your way with me as your guide to the basement. I would bring you downstairs because these are the most frequented rooms in our home. We often snack and watch shows together in the television room, which is in our basement. There are three rooms, stacked floor to ceiling with books, where I have spent countless hours reading and organizing my literary hoard. One of the rooms is my office, and it has an old wooden desk heaped with papers, books, and a few more books, if truth be told. I am confident that some of my kids are going to think back upon the old brick house we've lived in for thirteen years and think of their father's book obsession. They will likely remember watching *Alaska: The Last Frontier* and *Life Below Zero*, and they will remember their mom and dad's silly dream to one day own a farm. In many ways, I hope they remember the times I asked them to take the plastic garbage containers and collect loads of sticks and twigs at the end of fall, to ready ourselves with kindling for the coming winter. I don't know what they will remember, but the things that mattered most to us, things we did on a regular basis, will likely be a foundation for them that will show up in later years.

Maybe they will walk through a bookstore and suddenly see a book that I had next to my chair. I have memories like that that are so vivid for me from my youth. I can remember leaning against my father's chest as he read James Clavell's *Shogun* and *King Rat*. Those were good memories, and I hope I can give some of them to my children, as well. I have a number of memories of being taken to libraries and bookstores and reading *The Catcher in the Rye* at my father's house.

The other day, I was strolling about a massive record store in Pittsburgh, Pennsylvania. It is called Jerry's Records, and this guy has more records than you could ever imagine. Walking up and down the aisles of vinyl, I had a memory of an odd record my father had, which I listened to as a small child. It had a gigantic humpback whale on the cover, and it was simply the recorded sounds of whales in the water, moaning their mysterious songs to one another. Dad also had a whale tooth that I loved to examine and hold, especially while listening to the whale record. So I asked the guy working at Jerry's Records if they had anything with whale sounds, and sure enough, I found the exact same record. Talk about a walk down memory lane!

While I am sure my father had a number of different recollections he wishes I would have held on to, especially a fond appreciation for all of the museums he took me to, he didn't get to pick what would lodge into my brain. I won't be able to pick what my kids remember, and it is likely that they will be scarred for life from the amount of bookstores I dragged them to. What they will not be able to do is imagine that books were not important to their father. They won't be able to pretend that the faith was an occasional experience, nor will they be able to entertain the idea that their father was disinterested in their mother.

The other day, my neighbor had a funny run-in with my youngest son. He knew that one of my boys had a great love for pancakes, so he asked little Joe what it was that he liked. Joseph told my neighbor that he loved Legos, which really wasn't that surprising. Then my neighbor asked Joe what his mother liked, to which he responded, "My mom likes iced coffee." That also is very true! Then little Joe was asked what his dad liked, and Joe said, "My dad likes my mom."

I love that answer! What is the legacy I am leaving my kids? My greatest prayer is that it is the love I have for my faith, my wife, and my kids, and my desire to always grow in knowledge and understanding. I want to have only the good stick in their tiny little brains, but I am sure they will also remember the times I yelled at them for something their brother or sister really did, the days I was crazy about cleaning the house because we had company on the way, or the occasional words, which were certainly not French, and needing to be pardoned! God only knows what they will remember as adults, but I sure hope there is a lot of love in their recollections because that is what their mother and I have tried to do!

For Reflection

- What kind of a legacy are you leaving your children?
- Are there things you wished you had done differently over the years? If so, what might you start doing today to create a more positive legacy?
- If you were to ask your children what they remember most from their youth, what do you think they'd say?
- Now ask your children that question—is their response different from what you expected?

Chapter Fifteen

Be Holy, Be Happy

Over the years, many of our friends have struggled in their marriages. Many have wrestled through the difficult times, but a number of others felt their differences were irreconcilable. Some of these marriages ended in divorce, and others ended with the death of a spouse. We have friends who have gotten married later in life and friends who found spouses when it seemed certain they would end up as priests. We know a couple who both were discerning religious life but ended up married, and we even know a priest who was given permission by the Church to eventually become married. With such a wide range of life situations, there simply will never be one book that is perfect for every marital dynamic that is out there.

Some couples need serious counseling sessions to move past hurts and resentments, while some just need a little encouragement. We don't know where you are on your marriage journey, or what led you to pick up this book—or if it was just given to you as a gift from someone who was thinking of you—but we hope you found something in these pages that was practical and encouraging. We knew this work could not fill every gap, heal every heart, or answer every question, but we truly felt that if we could be honest and speak from our experiences that it just might work for the good. The greatest compliment that we will ever receive as authors is hearing that someone actually read the book and was encouraged by it. We pray that is the case for you. We have a long way to go and are trying to implement these principles into our own marriage, so let's pray for each other.

We are confident that God wants to remind all of us that marriage is a beautiful gift in which he moves and is present. Jesus was born to a married couple, his first miracle was performed at a marriage, and ultimately we get to spend eternity with him in a way that is best likened to the union and love found in holy matrimony. Be holy! Holiness is attractive, and holiness leads to happiness, peace, and joy.

For those of you who have had marriages that couldn't endure for any number of reasons, know that we would never want to present an attitude that is judgmental. We don't know what it has been like in your home, with your spouse, enduring your highs and lows, and we don't pretend to have all of the answers that you need. What we do have is our faith and the conviction that no regret is bigger than our God's healing and love. Know that Jesus wants you to have a holy, happy, thriving marriage even more than you do—and know that we are cheering you on!

Notes

1. Dietrich von Hildebrand, *Marriage the Mystery of Faithful Love* (Manchester, N.H.: Sophia Institute, 1991), p. xii (from the foreword by Alice von Hildebrand).

2. *Familiaris Consortio*, 6.

3. *Gaudium et Spes*, 4.

About the Authors

High-school sweethearts Chris and Linda Padgett have been married for more than twenty-four years and have nine children. Chris is a lay evangelist, author, musician, and teacher who travels the world giving missions and concerts. Linda is a blogger and has a ministry to women. Together, the Padgetts often lead marriage missions and retreats.